BORDER TOWNS BUSES OF LONDON COUNTRY TRANSPORT (NORTH OF THE THAMES) 1969–2019

Front cover: Ensignbus have been one of the main success stories in this area. They were the first company to introduce these Chinese-built BCI Enterprise buses. Eleven of these 10.8m two axle double-deck buses came in 2017, and No. 147 is about to enter Lakeside bus station on 5 October 2017.

Rear cover top: EOS were one of the shorter-lived companies, only operating between 2014-2018. TransBus Dart SLF 752 heads away from Epping station towards the High Street on a journey to Harlow in 2017.

Rear cover bottom: The Luton Busway, opened in 2013, is served not only by local services to Dunstable and Houghton Regis but also by express service F70 to Milton Keynes and F77 to Bletchley.

BORDER TOWNS BUSES OF LONDON COUNTRY TRANSPORT (NORTH OF THE THAMES) 1969–2019

MALCOLM BATTEN

PEN & SWORD
TRANSPORT

AN IMPRINT OF PEN & SWORD BOOKS LTD.
YORKSHIRE – PHILADELPHIA

First published in Great Britain in 2024 by
Pen and Sword Transport
An imprint of
Pen & Sword Books Ltd
Yorkshire - Philadelphia

ISBN 978 1 39909 609 6

Typeset in 11/14 Palatino
Typeset by SJmagic DESIGN SERVICES, India.

Printed and bound by Printworks Global Ltd, London/Hong Kong.

Pen & Sword Books Ltd incorporates the Imprints of Pen & Sword Books Archaeology, Atlas, Aviation, Battleground,
Discovery, Family History, History, Maritime, Military, Naval, Politics, Railways, Select, Transport, True Crime, Fiction,
Frontline Books, Leo Cooper, Praetorian Press, Seaforth Publishing, Wharncliffe and White Owl.

For a complete list of Pen & Sword titles please contact

PEN & SWORD BOOKS LIMITED
George House, Units 12 & 13, Beevor Street, Off Pontefract Road,
Barnsley, South Yorkshire, S71 1HN, England
E-mail: enquiries@pen-and-sword.co.uk
Website: www.pen-and-sword.co.uk

or

PEN AND SWORD BOOKS
1950 Lawrence Rd, Havertown, PA 19083, USA
E-mail: Uspen-and-sword@casematepublishers.com
Website: www.penandswordbooks.com

CONTENTS

INTRODUCTION

The mighty London Passenger Transport Board (trading as London Transport) was created in 1933. This had rights to run bus (and tram and trolleybus) services not only in the Greater London area (Central Area), but also extending to an area stretching up to a 25-mile radius from Charing Cross (Country Area). The main component of London Transport, the London General Omnibus Company, had established a network of routes south of London under the East Surrey name with a headquarters in Reigate. From 1929 they instigated the Green Line express services linking country towns to London and in most cases across to other country towns the other side of the metropolis. In 1932 they had amalgamated with the National Omnibus and Transport Co. Ltd north of London to form London General Country Services. The total London Passenger Transport Area (LPTA) extended north as far as Hitchin and Baldock, east to Brentwood, south to Crawley and Horsham and west to Windsor. Within this boundary was an area known as the 'Special Area'. Parts of this, mainly in the east and west, were coterminous with the boundary of the LPTA but fell short of this north and south. Within the Special Area the LPTB had monopoly powers except for long distance express services starting from outside the area. The routes and vehicles from other operators within the Special Area were taken over. Outside the special area, companies could also apply for licences to run services. At the LPTA boundary services could cross over, generally up to half a mile to reach a convenient terminal point, or up to ten miles (five miles in Kent) with agreement with the established operator.

By 1951, London Transport was making a deficit, and the Chambers' Report published in 1955 recommended that independent operators should be allowed to take over unremunerative LT routes, which happened in both Central and Country Areas. This also recommended improving the situation in the border towns to create inter-running arrangements, although little was done to this effect.

London Transport also ran the London Underground, whose lines acquired from the Metropolitan Railway extended as far as Verney Junction, Buckinghamshire, north of Aylesbury and beyond even the country bus area. Later, under the 1935 New Works Programme, the Central line would gain an extension from the LNER taking it to Epping and Ongar, at the outer limits of the Country Area in Essex.

There was a considerable degree of overlap between the red Central Area and green Country Area LT buses at the edges of Greater London, but what of the towns at the edge of the Country Area? Here, the Country Area buses would meet the bus companies whose operations extended across the rest of the counties of Essex, Hertfordshire, Bedfordshire, etc. In some cases, the town was at a node where more than one other company worked in. At Luton there was a municipally owned fleet, the only such example that LT encountered. Elsewhere, such as at Aylesbury, Windsor and Guildford, there were local independent operators who had a share in the town services.

The depth of the Country Area was more extensive north and south of London than was the case east and west. Indeed, in the east there was an unusual situation at Romford, a town within the Greater London area. Here the local services were provided by Central Area red buses, but despite there also being a Country Area garage in the town, the second largest operator was Eastern National, who came in from Southend, Chelmsford, etc and whose buses ran right through to Wood Green or London (Victoria or King's Cross).

This was not the only location where the red Central Area buses of London Transport met up with the companies from beyond the Country Area. The red buses had several routes that ran out into the Country Area and would also meet up with Eastern National at Brentwood and Ongar. In the west they reached Slough where they met Thames Valley who served Berkshire and part of South Buckinghamshire.

In 1969 you could get a Green Rover ticket for 7/- (adult) 3/6 (children) from Country Bus conductors any time at weekends and after 09.30 Monday-Friday. This gave a day's unlimited travel on over 1,500 miles of almost all Country Area routes (except a few works journeys) but not on Green Line services. A Weekender ticket for 25/- gave a Saturday/Sunday or Sunday/ Bank Holiday Monday unlimited travel on all Central Area, Country Area, Green Line and Underground services.

It would all change from January 1970 when the London Transport Country Area (including Green Line) along with 1,267 buses was transferred to the National Bus Company (NBC) to form a new company named London Country Bus Services (LCBS). The NBC had itself been created on 1 January 1969 under the 1968 Transport Act. This brought together the existing state-owned bus fleets such as Eastern National and United Counties with those formerly owned by the British Electric Traction (BET) Group such as Aldershot & District and Maidstone & District. Under National Bus Company ownership some neighbouring companies would be merged – Thames Valley was joined with Aldershot & District to form Alder Valley in January 1972.

At first under the NBC, routes remained largely as they had been before. But a number of factors would change this dramatically by the end of the 1980s. Increasing car ownership and changes to leisure travel were making many rural routes unprofitable and bus operators were seeking grant aid from local authorities to subsidise these. This aid was not always available, so some routes were cut back or withdrawn. The National Bus Company instigated a series of Market Analysis Project (MAP) surveys from 1978 onwards which reorganised route patterns and generally led to a reduction in the number of buses. However, some counties were able to fund special leisure services on Sundays to boost tourism.

When LCBS started, Green Line services had been worked by a mixture of the ageing although refurbished RF class, RMC and RCL Routemaster buses and the RC class of 1965 AEC Reliances. An early purchase was of the ninety-strong RP class of dual-purpose AEC Reliances to replace the crew-worked Routemasters on routes that were rapidly losing passengers as increasing car-ownership and traffic congestion made these services less attractive. The introduction of Leyland Nationals, which at first were basically buses with PVC seats, to Green Line routes did nothing to win back passengers. However, in 1977, under the direction of managing director Derek Fytche, LCBS began a policy, unusual for its time, of leasing rather than buying proper coaches in a successful scheme to upgrade the services.

For LCBS, there was some scope for new services, particularly to the expanding airports at Gatwick, Luton and Stanstead. But, until 1980, any new services had to be approved by the Traffic Commissioners and British Rail or other bus companies could object and block any perceived competition.

Long distance express services over thirty miles were deregulated under the Conservative government in 1980. One immediate consequence of this was a joint through service between Reading and Southend via London jointly operated by the two municipal fleets. They would later split into separate services to London. Deregulation now also allowed LCBS to further develop airport links and commuter services as a revitalisation of the Green Line brand.

London Transport had been placed under the ownership of the Greater London Council in 1970. In 1982, the GLC's decision to increase rates to fund the buses and Underground, the so-called 'Fares Fair' policy, was ruled illegal after a court challenge by Bromley Council. This resulted in fares being doubled, service cuts of 15 per cent, garage closures, and also the first withdrawals of Routemasters. The LT total bus fleet was reduced by some 600 vehicles.

Significantly, they withdrew from many of the routes running out beyond Greater London to places like Brentwood and Ongar. Some of these routes were taken over by the LCBS companies. They also later withdrew support for Green Line services in their area in June 1991.

Deregulation of bus services in October 1986 led to commercially registered routes being open to competition and other routes being put out to tender by the County Councils. The main commercially profitable routes were urban services, so competition sprang up in such places as Harlow, Luton and Stevenage. Often daytime services would be registered as commercial, but evening and Sunday services were not, so these would go out to tender and smaller companies with lower overheads would bid to run these. In Greater London a different system prevailed – open competition was not allowed but eventually all routes would be put out to tender.

In the new climate of deregulation and with the impending privatisation of NBC companies, some of the NBC companies were split up. The Secretary of State for Transport, Nicholas Ridley, declared that 'Size is seen as a hindrance to fair competition'. London Country Bus Services with 1,194 vehicles was considered too big and was split into four separate area companies on 7 September 1986. Alder Valley was also split back into separate parts as Alder Valley North and South from 1 January 1986.

The London Country companies plus Eastern National, Maidstone Borough Transport (Boro'Line) and numerous independents, some new to bus operation, won tenders for London bus routes. As these companies could initially keep their own liveries, you could soon see their buses across much of London. Mind you, it did look a bit odd to see buses proclaiming themselves as 'Boro'Line Maidstone' or 'Kentish Bus' in areas north of the Thames! London Country (South West) renamed themselves London & Country as a result of their involvement in London tendered work.

London Transport itself was replaced in 1984 by London Regional Transport, and in April 1985 new subsidiary companies London Buses Ltd and London Underground Ltd were set up. In April

1989, London Buses was split into eleven regional operating units, plus London Coaches who ran the sightseeing operation. This was in preparation for eventual privatisation in the 1990s. These London bus companies, including newly created 'low-cost' units, could tender for services not only for routes in Greater London but also for routes outside the Greater London area. This was more the case in Kent and Surrey at that time, but more recently tendering changes have witnessed the return of red London buses to Thurrock and Brentwood.

Privatisation of the National Bus Company from 1986-8 and the London Buses companies in the 1990s led to further changes in the names and ownership of bus companies. Things got more complicated as London Country (North West) was bought by Luton and District in 1990 – a company hived off from United Counties in 1986. Earlier that year they had taken much of the Stevenage area from Sovereign – a company split off from London Country (North East).

Consolidation since then has seen the emergence of national bus groups – Stagecoach, First Group, Arriva and Go-Ahead, replacing the old names and liveries. Eventually all of the old London Country successor companies fell into the hands of Arriva, but the boundaries were now different. Thus, Arriva the Shires & Essex comprised both parts of the former London Country (North East) and (North West) areas but also part of Luton & District, which was originally United Counties. Arriva itself has been owned by the German Deutsche Bahn since 2010.

The major bus groups also acquired, directly or indirectly, many of the smaller companies that had grown up to challenge them on commercial routes or to take over routes that had been abandoned by the larger companies.

The new Millennium coincided with a change in ownership for London's bus services. From 3 July 2000, a new Mayor of London was appointed, who took over responsibility for London Bus Services Ltd and a new regulatory authority called Transport for London (TfL).

Overall service levels have declined since the 1970s, and many smaller villages previously

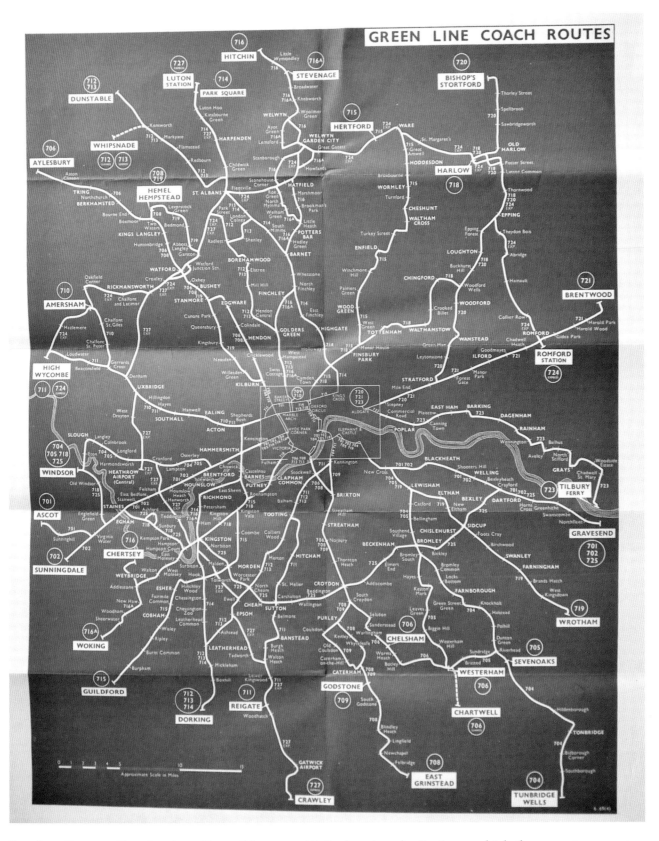

London Country Bus Services Green Line map 1970, showing the limits to which these routes ran at the time of acquisition from London Transport.

served no longer receive a regular service, or any service at all. Deregulation ended the ability to cross-subsidise loss-making routes from more profitable routes. Government policy leading to local council budget cuts has resulted in reductions in funding for subsidies so again more cuts to services or cheaper options such as community minibuses replacing regular routes.

Above left: London Transport Green Line map 1969.

Above right: London Country Bus Services Green Line map 1970, featuring an RC class, then the newest coaches in the fleet.

However, continued retrenchment by the major companies and cutbacks in council support have given an opportunity for new independent companies to fill the gaps. Some of these have now become quite well-established, significant companies – for instance Ensignbus, originally dealers, are now the major operator in the Thurrock area of Essex. They were awarded Top Independent Operator in the 2012, 2014 and 2019 UK Bus Awards. But there have been other independent companies that have found the going tougher than they expected and have quickly fallen by the wayside. We have even had the reappearance of a municipal fleet on the borders. Reading Transport, one of the few remaining municipally owned companies, has expanded in recent years, taking over a former Green Line route into London and local routes into Slough.

This book takes the form of an anti-clockwise tour around the perimeter of the London Country area north of the Thames, featuring a number of key towns starting at Tilbury and ending at High Wycombe. A companion book will continue from Slough and Windsor then south of the Thames through Guildford, Crawley and East Grinstead to finish at Gravesend and Bluewater. They cover a period from 1969 to 2019, illustrating some of the many changes to bus companies that have occurred during this period. It does not claim to be fully comprehensive in illustrating all of the bus companies that have served the featured towns. There are also other companies that have come and gone, serving other towns within the former London Country area – Watford, Hemel Hempstead, Welwyn, etc – but these have been considered as outside of the remit of this selection.

All photographs are by the author except where stated.

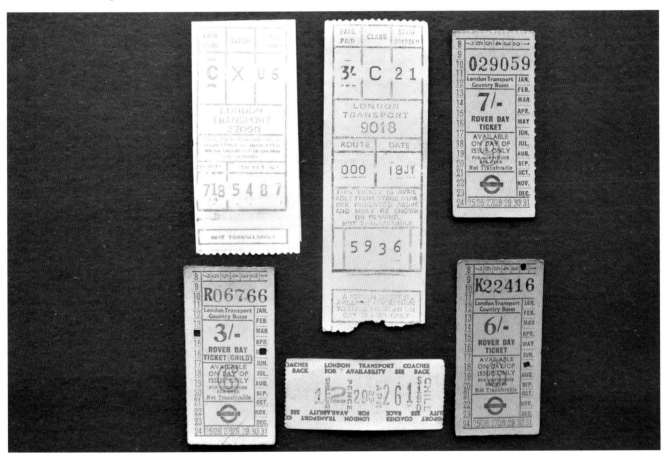

London Transport Country Area tickets 1960s.

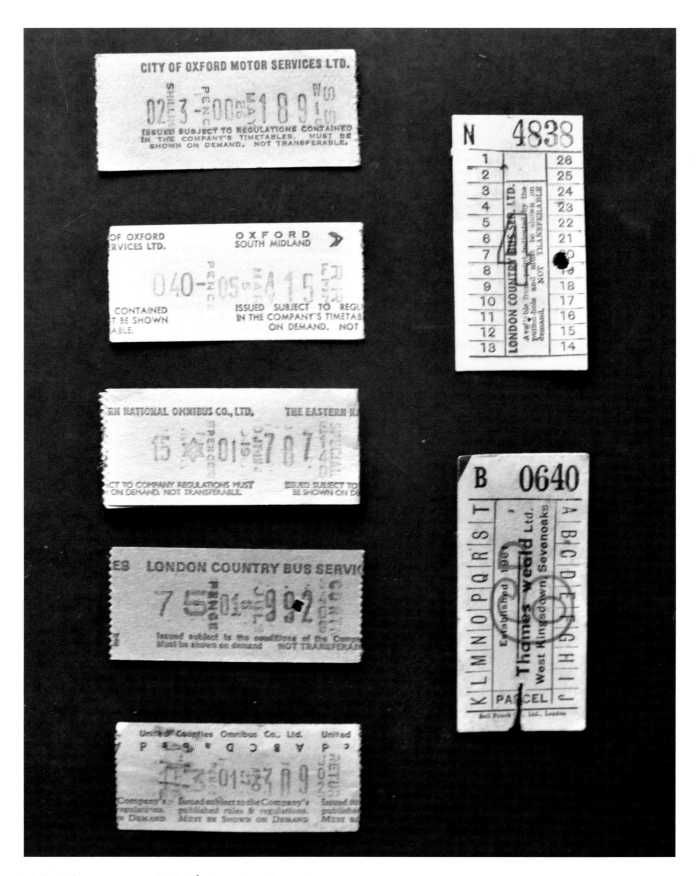

Tickets from companies in the 1960s and 1970s.

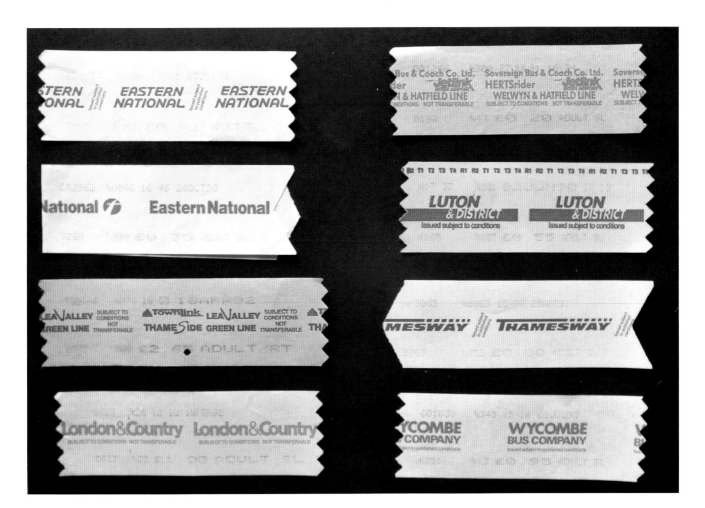

Above: Tickets from main companies in the 1980s and 1990s.

Right: Tickets from independent companies in the 1980s and 1990s.

Tickets from national group companies in the 2000s.

THURROCK: TILBURY, GRAYS AND LAKESIDE

When London Transport was set up, the LPTA boundary cut through the middle of Grays, leaving the east side with LT and the west side with the Eastern National Omnibus Company (ENOC). In 1951, the local ENOC services, garage and buses transferred to London Transport. The routes were revised in 1952 and renumbered into the LT 300s series for country routes north of the Thames.

When LCBS was split up, this area became part of the territory of London Country (North East). This was the last of the NBC subsidiaries to be privatised with the operations going to AJS Holdings in April 1988. The garages went to a separate owner, Parkdale Holdings, who were keen to sell off those located in prime town centre sites.

AJS sold most of its Essex operations to its chairman in late 1990 while retaining twenty-nine vehicles and five services at Grays, this becoming the Lynton Travel Group though retaining the County Bus name by then in use. Both companies shared the Grays garage and the ThameSide fleetname Lynton Travel was bought by West Midlands Travel in 1994, and then sold to the Cowie Group – who at that time already owned Grey-Green and Leaside in east/north-east London – in 1996. Cowie subsequently bought out the British Bus group and renamed themselves Arriva at the end of 1997.

The Lakeside Shopping Centre opened in 1990, making a major difference in shopping patterns for the Thurrock area. Previously, Grays had been the local shopping hub, while Romford market was the regional centre. Now Lakeside took on that role, and the bus station provided there was the focus for local operations. Longer distance excursions worked in from such areas as East London with a shopper's special route 723X from Stratford, four journeys on Saturdays only. With the proximity of the Dartford tunnel, excursions also came in from the Kent side. This ended when another major shopping centre opened at Bluewater on the Kent side in March 1999.

Ensign Bus Company had been dealers established in 1972, originally based at Grays, and also operating works contracts. Bus operations started from 28 October 1985 with sightseeing tours in London. Their first London tendered contract came in June 1986. With the opening of Lakeside in 1990, they introduced route 565 from Romford to Lakeside. The London bus operations were sold to CNT Holdings Hong Kong, in January 1991, trading as Capital Citybus. The dealership and sightseeing and rail replacement businesses continued however and in 2004 bus services restarted around Thurrock, starting with route X80 to Gravesend via Bluewater via the Dartford crossings. The reason for this was that Ensign had won a contract to supply up to fourteen buses a day for a rail replacement contract lasting twelve months between Gravesend and Strood while the Higham tunnel was refurbished. The buses had to get to Kent via the Dartford bridge and tunnel, with tolls for buses not in passenger service costing £2 per crossing while those in passenger service (even if no passengers were on board) were free. Hence the X80 was registered, becoming a commercial success. Other routes started in competition with Arriva from July 2006. The attractive, reliable services running seven days a week soon began to attract customers away from their cars and within six years the four trunk routes were carrying around 10,000 passengers a day.

In 2006, a projected South Essex Rapid Transit (SERT) scheme was proposed for Southend, Basildon and Thurrock. Buses would have had dedicated lanes where possible and priority at traffic lights with opening planned for 2012. One route would have linked Lakeside Shopping Centre to Basildon via Grays. The other would have been between Southend seafront and Southend Airport. The project had been allocated £51m but local authorities were seeking more, including £10m to begin infrastructure construction. In October 2010, the Department for Transport placed this project in the pre-qualification pool, meaning it had the least chance of being funded. The scheme was turned down by the transport secretary Justine Greening, who asked councils to provide more evidence that the project would constitute value for money.

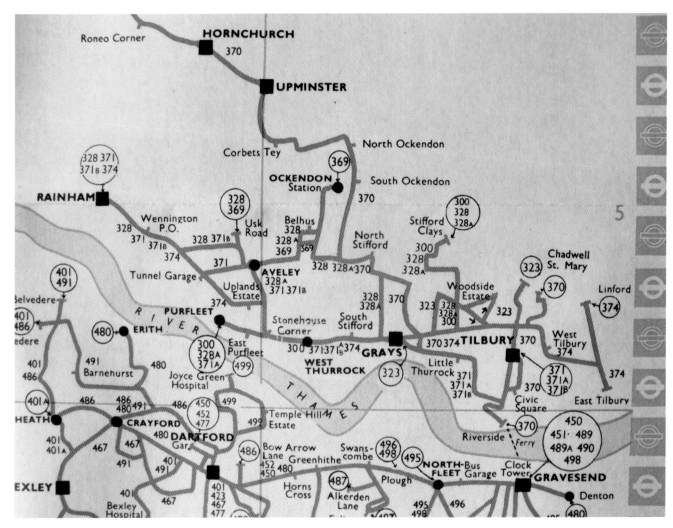

Thurrock area Country Area services 1969. London Transport produced free maps of their Central and Country Area services but these did not show the routes of the other operators they met up with.

Above: Tilbury Ferry was the terminus for London Transport Green Line route 723 from London Aldgate via East Ham and Grays. Here, RMC1497 stands in the company of green RT4756 on route 370 to Romford on 12 June 1969. Both vehicles are based at Grays garage. From 1 January 1970 the green country buses and Green Line services passed to the National Bus Company as London Country Bus Services.

Below: Also at Tilbury Ferry on the same day is Eastern National Bristol FLF6B No. 2794 (BVX 670B) on route 53 which will go all the way through to Colchester where this bus was based.

Above: Tilbury Riverside station alongside the Passenger Landing Stage with its Ocean Liner Terminal (now London International Cruise Terminal) and ferry stage closed on 29 November 1992. Since then, a connecting bus service has linked Tilbury Town station with the ferry, which continues to run (now only Mondays–Saturdays) across to Gravesend. In 2017 this was provided by Ensignbus with this branded Dart which also served a local housing estate and Asda store on the return journey.

Opposite above: A pair of London Country RCL Routemasters parked up in Grays garage on 4 April 1976. The RCLs had originally been at Romford garage (RE) for Green Line routes 721 and 722 but London Country quickly replaced these with one-person operated single-deckers and downgraded them to bus work, before eventually selling their Routemasters back to London Transport. The 370 had also been cut back from Tilbury Ferry to Grays in May 1973.

Opposite below: London Country RCL2251 pulls out of Grays bus station on local route 323 on 17 February 1978.

Above: Eastern National still had a presence in Grays when this photo of Bristol FLF6LX No. 2927 was taken on 23 March 1979. Based at Basildon garage, it is working through to Southend and carries overall advertising for a Tesco store at Pitsea. Note the unusual position for the fleetname and National Bus symbol!

Opposite above: County Bus was the name for the eastern part of London Country (North East) when the company was divided in January 1989. They adopted local area fleetnames and ThameSide was the appropriate choice for these parts. SNB296, a 1977 Leyland National, was at Grays in March 1990.

Opposite below: Harris Bus Company was a subsidiary of Frank Harris (Coaches) Ltd who had been running coaches locally since 1923. They moved significantly into bus operation at deregulation on 1 October 1986 and soon became the major provider in Thurrock. Leaving Grays for Chadwell St. Mary in March 1990 is G316 YHJ, an Optare bodied DAF bought for new service 303 Chadwell St. Mary–Romford.

Above: A most unusual choice of vehicle for bus work was this Harris Bus Bova coach acquired in 1989. Although no blind display was fitted, the vehicle was fitted with bus style jackknife doors and was painted in the blue and cream bus livery. August 1990.

Opposite above: The opening of the Lakeside Shopping Centre in 1990 brought a new focus to bus operations in Thurrock. Harris Bus was well placed to capitalise on this, and double-deck vehicles were employed on local routes and a car park service. This is a former Northampton Bristol VR with Alexander bodywork on 18 April 1992.

Opposite below: Lakeside became a regional shopping centre, and before the equivalent Bluewater centre opened on the Kent side of the Thames there were excursions across via the Dartford crossings. On the same day, Kentish Bus 11, KBC 193, a 1983 MCW Metroliner coach acquired from Western Scottish in 1990, leaves the bus station to park up having arrived on route 722.

Above: When Ensignbus sold their bus services and vehicles to the CNT Group of Hong Kong in December 1990, the company was renamed Capital Citybus the following year. As well as London tendered services, the company ran a number of commercial services including the 565 from Romford to Lakeside. Alexander-bodied Leyland Olympian 172, seen at Lakeside on 18 April 1992, was acquired from Highland Scottish in 1992. Capital Citybus was taken over by FirstGroup in July 1998 and rebranded First Capital, but they withdrew from the Essex commercial work and these routes were taken over by Ensignbus.

Opposite above: Eastern National was sold to its management on 23 December 1986. Then it was sold on to Badgerline Holdings on 12 April 1990. The fleet was then split into two parts from 29 July 1990 with the southern part serving south Essex and London tendered services becoming Thamesway. The Badgerline Group merged with GRT Bus Group in June 1995 to become FirstBus plc. Thamesway Dennis Dart/Plaxton N964 CPU is route branded for route 100 which was the successor to the onetime 53, now running from Lakeside to Chelmsford. Taken in 1996.

Opposite below: Thamesway Volvo/Plaxton coach N613 APU on City Saver route S1 in 1996. This route was introduced from 6 July 1992, running Mondays-Fridays from Southend and Basildon to London (Piccadilly) via Lakeside, Dagenham, East Ham and Aldgate. Frequency was hourly off-peak with additional variant journeys in peak hours as routes S2 and S3; this was in competition with Southend Transport services. Nineteen of these Volvo coaches entered service in 1995.

Above: Harris Bus introduced a new livery in 1997 when they also won some London bus contracts. However, P318 KTW is branded for the Lakeside Link services L1-4 running from towns in north Kent. This is one of a pair of DAF DB250RS buses with Northern Counties Palatine II H47/30F bodies bought in 1996, following an earlier example in 1995. This was taken on 15 March 1997. Harris Bus would later get into financial difficulties with their London contracts and were placed in receivership in December 1999.

Opposite above: County Bus operated a number of commercial routes by agreement with London Regional Transport including the 373 from Romford to Lakeside on which this 1996 Dennis Dart route branded as 'The Lakeside Connection' is seen departing from the Lakeside bus station in 1977. County Bus had been sold to the Cowie Group in 1996, thus bringing it into the same ownership group as Grey-Green and Leaside Buses in London.

Opposite below: Town & Country were a new company that started up in 1998, buying four second-hand Dennis Darts for route 20 Lakeside-Tilbury. They then saw major expansion from 11 December 1999 when they took over Ensignbus routes 324,325,348 and 509 along with almost thirty buses. However, this would be short-lived as services 20 Lakeside-Tilbury, 324 Romford-Lakeside-Bluewater and 348 Romford-Chadwell St. Mary were all acquired by Arriva East Herts & Essex from 5 October 2000. The 509 Stratford-Bluewater had ceased after 7 April 2000 by which time it had gone down to just one round trip. With the demise of Town & Country on 20 October 2006, routes and school contracts were reassigned by Thurrock Council to a mixture of Arriva, Blue Triangle, Clintona, Ensignbus, First Essex and Harris Bus.

Above: On 14 October 1997 the Cowie Group was rebranded as Arriva. The former County Bus operations became Arriva East Herts & Essex Ltd. A new nationwide corporate livery was introduced, and this is displayed by 3389, a 1997 Dennis Dart SLF with Plaxton Pointer B39F bodywork. It carries route branding for Thurrock routes 377 and 383. 2 December 2006.

Opposite above: Ensignbus restarted commercial operations in the Thurrock area in 2004 starting with route X80 to Bluewater and Gravesend via the Dartford crossings. Other routes started in competition with Arriva from July 2006. This Dennis Dart SLF/Plaxton is leaving Lakeside for Bluewater in 2006 but the bus is route branded for Thurrock local routes 77 and 83 competing with Arriva's 377 and 383. Route branding was dropped once the number of routes increased. The X80 has continued hourly ever since but since 2006 only as far as Bluewater.

Opposite below: Blue Triangle Plaxton bodied Dart DP189 at Thurrock Lakeside bus station on a 372 journey to Hornchurch on 22 July 2006. The 372 was a part replacement of the 324 from 4 January 2003, running between Lakeside and Hornchurch as part of the TfL network. On 29 June 2007 the Go-Ahead Group announced that they had expanded their presence in East London by paying £12m for Blue Triangle Buses and its local bus operations. The deal included sixty-eight buses, the Rainham depot, eight TfL contracts, nine Essex contracts and rail replacement work. Like the Docklands company bought earlier, the name would be retained and the business run as an autonomous unit within Go-Ahead London.

Above: Route 370, now Romford–Thurrock Lakeside, had started out as a London Transport Country Area route from Romford to Tilbury Ferry, passing in turn to London Country and County Bus. It became part of the TfL network in November 2007 by which time it was being worked by Arriva Southern Counties from their Grays garage. It was the last TfL route to retain vehicles not in a red livery (i.e. Arriva corporate blue/white) until new London specification Alexander Dennis Enviro200 Darts came in 2008. One of these departs from Lakeside on 6 December 2008. Grays garage now operates as part of Arriva London and double-deckers have since taken over.

Opposite above: First Essex is the successor to Eastern National's one-time route 53 with route 100 Lakeside-Basildon. Since 2013, nineteen of these Volvo 7900H hybrid buses have worked the route. The Department for Transport provided seventy per cent of the purchase price for these buses, the first of their type to enter service in Britain. Since late 2017, a revised City Country Connections livery has been applied to these buses as seen here. The route previously continued to Chelmsford but was divided at Basildon.

Opposite below: Approaching Lakeside is one of a batch of ten Volvo B9TL buses with Optare Olympus bodies bought new by Ensignbus in 2008. This is on the hourly cross-river X80 service to Bluewater. Ensignbus vehicles do not carry commercial advertising.

Pioneered by Ensignbus are these Chinese-built BCI Enterprise buses. Eleven of these 10.8m two axle double-deck buses came in 2017, and No. 147 is about to enter the bus station on 5 October of that year. These have an in-line Cummins 6.7litre six-cylinder engine. All Thurrock local services are now with Ensignbus, Arriva only working TfL contract routes 370 and 372.

Ensignbus have a large fleet of heritage buses and a popular event since 2005 has been the annual Running Day, usually held on the first Saturday of December when the fleet, along with guest vehicles, take to the roads. The routes tend to vary each year but include services to Gravesend via the Dartford Crossings and to Upminster. The 2016 event took place in excellent sunny weather and Ensignbus's former London Transport RT8 departs Lakeside for Upminster with a full load of enthusiasts. In February 2023 Ensignbus was acquired by First Group, although the heritage fleet was not included in the sale.

ROMFORD

As mentioned in the introduction, at Romford, Eastern National buses, which ran throughout Essex, met up directly with the red London Transport buses. Indeed, they came right into London to King's Cross or Victoria. This was a legacy from when London Transport was set up. While all companies within its area were taken over, those at the perimeter or running in from beyond were not. City Coaches of Brentwood, on the perimeter, had a route from Southend to Wood Green, where they also had a garage. In February 1952, the services of City Coach Co. Ltd of Brentwood passed to Westcliff-on-Sea Motor Services who in turn were acquired by Eastern National in 1955. The Wood Green garage was closed and the terminus of the half-hourly route 251 changed to Walthamstow Central in 1981, providing connections with the Victoria Line. Route 251 ceased in June 1997 when replaced in part by the shorter 551.

The London Transport garage (RE) had come with the business of Hillman Coaches and was the base for Green Line vehicles on routes 721, 722, seasonal 726 and later 724, but did not operate any green country bus routes. London Transport had red bus garages at North Street, Romford (NS) which still remains in 2023 and at Hornchurch (RD), closed in 1988.

Romford market was a major Christmas shopping destination for south-east Essex shoppers until the Lakeside Shopping Centre in Thurrock opened in 1990.

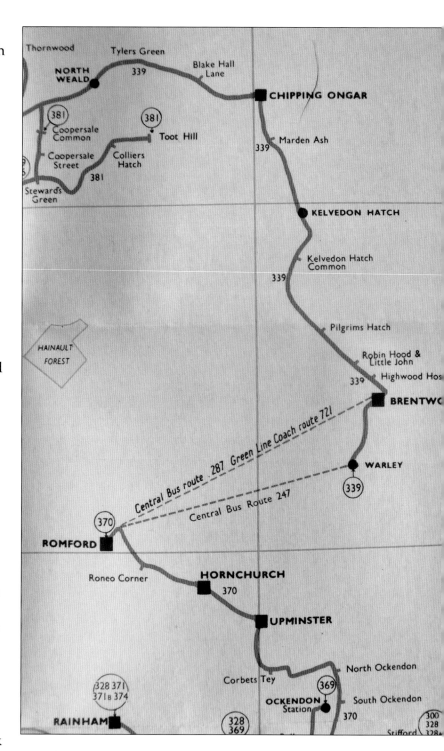

Romford and Brentwood area Country Area services 1969.

Above: Eastern National Bristol FLF6LX No. 2988 of Chelmsford garage lays over before working on route 351 for Chelmsford on 9 June 1969. Note the rear wheel covers – a feature also found on London Transport buses in the 1960s but removed in the 1970s.

Below: The Leyland National was designed with the National Bus Company and became a standard in NBC fleets. London Country began to allocate some to Green Line work, beginning with route 721 in February 1973. However, although painted in the new NBC 'dual purpose' livery and lettered Green Line, these had PVC bus seats, well below the standard passengers were used to on the RP class used beforehand in 1972 and the RCL Routemasters before that. LNC45 loads for Brentwood in Romford on 31 March 1973. In 1972, the route had a Monday-Saturday off-peak frequency of every 15 minutes and journey time of 1 hour 22 minutes. Despite this, the route was withdrawn in 1977 and Romford garage was closed.

GREEN LINE COACH
721

LONDON (Aldgate)
Stratford, Forest Gate
Ilford, Romford
BRENTWOOD

TIMETABLE AND FARES
1st January, 1972

London Country Bus Services Ltd.
Bell Street, Reigate, Surrey RH2 7LE
Tel. Reigate 42411

Left: LCBS Green Line route 721 leaflet 1972.

Below: An early purchase by London Country was the ninety strong RP class of Park Royal bodied AEC Reliances for Green Line work. RP41 of Staines garage has arrived at Romford on 11 September 1974 on the radial route 724 to Romford from Staines via Heathrow Airport. This route had originally been introduced in 1966 as High Wycombe to Romford but was amended in 1972. The RP class had previously been on the 721 until that route received Leyland Nationals. The 724 was withdrawn between Harlow and Romford from 20 May 1978, this section being replaced by the 712.

Opposite above: The RMC and RCL Routemasters displaced from Green Line work by LCBS from 1972 replaced RTs on bus work. RMC1507, now in NBC leaf green livery, is on the 370 at Romford. This location at St. Edwards Way near the market was ideal for photography in the mornings and most routes stopped here. Romford market drew shoppers from a wide area as evident by the market day crowds patiently queuing for buses on 11 September 1974.

Below: Eastern National had an hourly limited stop route X10 from London's Victoria Coach Station to Southend via Romford. In 1971, the company gained a batch of fifteen Bristol VRs from Scottish operator Alexander Midland, which initially retained their former owner's blue livery. One of these, No. 3007, loads at Romford in 1974 on the 400, which was the new number for the X10 from April 1971.

Above: Since 1967, Thames Weald of West Kingsdown, Sevenoaks had operated a 'Tunnel Express' service through the Dartford Tunnel, following London Transport's withdrawal of such services. This ran daily from Sevenoaks to Romford. In 1971, some journeys were extended from Sevenoaks to Crawley but this extension ended in January 1974. The largest vehicle used was this Bedford VAS with Plaxton body seen on 6 June 1975.

Opposite above: By the mid-1970s the Bristol VR had become a standard type for most National Bus Company fleets. However, London Country only took one batch, in 1977. These were built to full-height specification and replaced the RMCs and RCLs on route 370. BT2 lays over at the Romford LCBS garage with LT DMS662 on 8 June 1977. These vehicles only had a short life with LCBS, being transferred to Bristol in 1980.

Opposite below: Eastern National upgraded route 400 with some new VRs in the latest NBC 'dual purpose' style livery. No. 3067 is well laden as it arrives in Romford on 13 April 1984, where most passengers will probably alight to indulge in market day shopping. The bus will continue to London King's Cross, which had replaced Victoria Coach Station as the terminus since May 1973.

Above: Thames Weald's route from Sevenoaks to Romford still continued, albeit with frequency reductions. From December 1982 it had only run Wednesday-Saturday. PKR 399W was a 1981 built former demonstrator, a Dodge S66C with 27 seat Rootes body, taken on 7 August 1985. Thames Weald would cease trading in 1998 when the proprietor, Dr Nesbitt Heffernan, by then in his 80s, retired having been refused a renewal of his PSV driving licence on health grounds. At the end it was running between Dartford and Southend.

Opposite above: Eastern National 1055 was a 1981 built Bedford YMQS with Wadham Stringer 33 seat body. It was taken on 6 September 1985 on route 347 in Romford. This route had been introduced on 25 July 1981 to part replace LT route 247 Epping–Brentwood. Unusually, it was at first jointly worked by ENOC and LT on Mondays–Saturdays, although there was no inter-availability of tickets, but from 4 September it was run only Mondays–Fridays by ENOC.

Opposite below: In 1981, Bordabus was formed as an association between G.F. Stubbington (t/a Dorayme Travel) and Lewington Coach Hire of Abridge. In October 1981, they introduced a route from Waltham Cross to Romford with one journey on Wednesdays and Fridays (market days) only. This later increased to five journeys a day and included Saturdays. On 15 December 1984, GSL 896N, an Alexander bodied Daimler Fleetline ex-Tayside No. 168, departs from Romford.

Above: 1985 saw the start of tendering out London Regional Transport routes. In the first round of tendering, Eastern National won two routes from 13 July, the W9 Enfield–Southgate, and the 193 Romford–Emerson Park (County Hall Estate). At first, Bristol VRs were used on the 193 with LRT roundels applied. London Transport had been using Leyland Titans on the route since September 1982. Thus, the Eastern National presence in Romford expanded. From 2 August 1986, route 193 was revised to incorporate the 256 and an express section was introduced between Romford and Hornchurch. Eastern National replaced the Bristol VRs with Ford Transit minibuses and the route was branded as the 'Hornchurch Hoppa'. 14 August 1986.

Opposite above: By February 1989 the contract for the Sunday service on route 500 to Harlow which on weekdays was run by London Country (North East) had passed to Blue Triangle whose former DMS404 is seen at Romford on 5 February. Note the lack of passengers waiting for this or any other service. Sunday shopping was not to come in until July 1994, making such journeys uneconomic to register commercially. Blue Triangle was to become a major player in the next decade. In 1988 the Sunday contract had been with London Buses (see p. 81).

Opposite below: A new innovation for 1990 (and repeated in 1991) was Essex County Council Summer Sunday (and Bank Holiday Mondays) 'heritage' leisure route 612 which ran all the way from Romford to Colchester in some 3.5 hours. On its (indirect) way it passed the East Anglian Railway Museum at Chappell and the Colne Valley Railway at Castle Hedingham. It was run by Blue Triangle who usually put out former London Transport RF401. The bus is seen leaving Romford on 17 June. The passengers are probably mainly transport enthusiasts. A similar 'heritage' working had taken place in 1988-9 between Harlow and Great Yeldham on which two RTs had been used (see p. 81).

Above: Blue Triangle also won other Essex contracts including route 265 to West Horndon. Here, former London Transport Leyland National LS174 is at Romford station. This vehicle has now been preserved by the London Bus Company/London Vintage Bus Hire, the successors to Blue Triangle. 21 March 1991.

Below: London Country had been split into four parts in September 1986, with London Country (North East) being further split in two in January 1989. Now as County Bus, former London Country TL31 was a 1982 Leyland Tiger with ECW C49F bodywork, originally a Green Line coach. In 1993, when this was seen at Romford station, it was working route 500 to Stanstead Airport, and like many of the batch had been given an overall advertising livery.

Above: Nelson, Wickford, trading as NIBS, built up a number of routes around Basildon and the surrounding parts of Essex. They also gained an Essex contract into Romford where this Mercedes-Benz was taken in March 1995.

Below: Sporting a new style livery with evidence of ownership by the Badgerline group, this Plaxton-bodied Dennis Dart of Thamesway was taken on the same day in March 1995.

Above: Four low-floor Wright bodied Dennis Lances for County Bus were bought with assistance from Essex County Council for route 502 Romford-Harlow in 1994. Essex CC also helped fund four low-floor buses for Southend Transport and two for Hedingham Omnibuses under the same arrangement, with the vehicles to be kept on the specified routes for at least two years. These replaced the TL series of Leyland Tigers seen earlier.

Opposite above: The end of an era came on 6 May 2000 when First Thamesway withdrew the remaining section of route 251 Walthamstow–Basildon. This was the successor to the erstwhile City Coaches, then Eastern National route from Wood Green-Southend. It had switched from Wood Green to Walthamstow Central in June 1981. Seen in 1996, this Leyland Olympian/ECW carries the older style of livery.

Opposite below: Eastern National 1003 was a 1983 Leyland Tiger TRBTL11/2R with Duple DP47F bodywork that had started out with Yorkshire Rider as their No. 1653. Here at Romford station in 1996 working on the 351 to Braintree, it is route branded for a service from Southend to Stanstead Airport and Bishop's Stortford.

Above: Thurrock Lakeside gained a rival in 1999 when the Bluewater Shopping Centre opened near Greenhithe, Kent on 16 March. Routes 324 and 348 had been worked by Capital Citybus, but when First Capital took over, they withdrew from the Essex commercial work and these routes were taken over by Ensignbus. Route 348 was extended to go on to Gravesend. A Metrobus 2, this one originating with Northern General, promotes both routes as it loads in Romford on 3 November 1999. However, in December 1999, Ensignbus sold these routes to a new company, Town & Country Buses.

Opposite above: After withdrawal of Thamesway route 251, the Romford–Basildon section was replaced by the 751. First Thamesway Dart 712, suitably branded, lays over at Romford station on 4 November. This route would be withdrawn itself in a round of cuts in March 2005.

Opposite below: Arriva the Shires & Essex route 500 was withdrawn between Ongar and Romford on 5 July 2008. The London section had been run under a London Local Service Agreement. It was replaced by Go-Ahead London (Blue Triangle) one-bus route 375 as far as Passingford Bridge which is still running in 2023. The last remaining vestige of a service between Romford and Epping by 2018 was the one daily trip each way Monday-Friday on route 575 from Romford to Harlow via Abridge and Epping. Go-Ahead London's PVL392 leaves the Brewery at Romford with the 13.00 hours return trip on 1 October 2018. This was withdrawn from 27 August 2021.

BRENTWOOD

Brentwood was the furthest point due east reached by London Transport, both red and green buses, and also Green Line coaches. The first town beyond the boundary of the London Borough of Havering, the main operator was Eastern National who had a garage located here (coded BD).

Above: Eastern National 2535 a 1959 Bristol LD5G of Brentwood garage works a local service on 6 June 1975.

Opposite above: On the same day, Bristol MW5G No. 1349 stands at Brentwood garage.

Opposite below: Frontrunner were a subsidiary of East Midland Buses from Chesterfield. From deregulation, they gained some Essex contracts including local routes around Brentwood not registered as commercial by ENOC and route 347 from Brentwood–Romford. Also gained were the 250 and 251 at Loughton, previously worked by Sampsons. No. 5, a 1974 Bristol RELH6L with ECW DP47F body, is seen in Brentwood on 19 December 1986. While some vehicles gained 'Frontrunner' names, others retained East Midland branding. From 24 September 1988, Frontrunner also gained London routes 248 and 252 at Romford. The Frontrunner regime on Romford routes 248 and 252 did not last long, for from 30 June 1989 these routes passed to Ensignbus, following the Stagecoach Group's acquisition of East Midland. The Essex contracts and depots would pass to County Bus in July.

Above: Harris Bus began operating on 1 April 1986, when route 269 Grays–Brentwood was taken over from Ingatestone Coaches. Other services were taken over from London Country on Essex County Council contracts from the start of deregulation on 1 October 1986 and further contracts followed later. They took the Monday-Saturday route 265 from Brentwood to Bulphan on an Essex County Council contract. Seen here is a 1988 Leyland Swift with Wadham Stringer B37F body, one of a pair bought new. 21 October 1988.

Opposite above: Although London Buses had withdrawn from serving Brentwood in 1981 (see p. 40) their red buses did make a brief return in 1989 when they won Essex tendered route 699. This was a summer Sundays only service from Romford to Upminster via the South Weald Country Park and Brentwood. Tickets were not valid for journeys wholly within the Greater London area. A minibus was sufficient and here MCW Metrorider MR16 is departing from Romford on 8 October. The service only lasted the one season.

Opposite below: Clintona were a long-established minibus operator specialising in providing accessible vehicles for disabled people. They also had some local route contracts at various times in Loughton, Brentwood, Harlow and Thurrock. On 18 June 2005 Mercedes-Benz 0814D / Plaxton B33F SF04 HXL is on their route 261 to Blackmore.

Above: First Essex Dennis Dart 46804 works a local service in June 2005.

Below: In an unusual start date, from Boxing Day 2005, red buses made a return to Brentwood when the contract for new route 498 Romford–Brentwood was awarded to Arriva Kent Thameside. This replaced First Essex Buses routes 351 and 551 who withdrew because their buses did not meet TfL's environmental requirements and they did not consider it justified the cost of new buses. Vehicles were provided from Arriva Southend's Grays garage. Alexander bodied DAF SB250 6223 was on the stand at Brentwood on 11 February 2006. New VDL SB120 single-deckers ordered for the route later took over. The route has since become worked by Stagecoach East London on retendering.

Above: Amber Coaches, Rayleigh, mainly worked on contract, schools and private hire duties until 2013 when they took over routes 261,265,268 and 269 in the Brentwood and Thurrock areas. SK07 HLN, an Alexander Dennis E200Dart, takes on passengers in the High Street during 2014. The company would later lose these routes.

Below: Ensignbus 729 (Y329 FJN), an ex-Stagecoach London Dennis Dart SLF/Alexander, was painted in this commemorative City Coach Company livery in 2012 to mark the sixtieth anniversary of the end of City Coach Company when it was taken over by Westcliff-on-Sea Motor Services in 1952, who would soon afterwards themselves be absorbed into Eastern National.

Ensignbus

From 29th May 2018

21/X21 Brentwood - Ongar via Pilgrims Hatch

81/X81 Brentwood - Hutton via Shenfield

21 Ongar Four Wantz

Ensignbus   701   PX61 AXZ

WINNER of 'Small Bus Operator of the Year'
(RouteONE Awards 2017, Medium Bus Operator 2016 & 2017)

WINNER of 'Top Independent Bus Operator of the Year'
(UK Bus Awards 2012 & 2014, finalists 2015, 2016 & 2017)

Above: Stephensons operate services extensively across much of Essex and had a small presence in Brentwood on routes 71 and 72. This Alexander Dennis E20D was at the station in 2019.

Opposite: Ensignbus leaflet 2018.

Opposite above: Nelson's Independent Bus Services (NIBS) of Wickford was bought by Stephensons in October 2018. They were already running route 269 from Brentwood-Grays when, in 2019, they arranged to take over the working of Brentwood routes 21 to Ongar, and local routes 31 and 81 from Ensignbus. Mostly Alexander Dennis vehicles are used, but the fleet does also include this 'wheel forward' Wright Streetlite at the station on route 31 in 2020.

Opposite below: Brentwood Community Transport operate a handful of buses including this Bluebird Tucana seen in 2019.

Right: NIBS Buses Leaflet 2021.

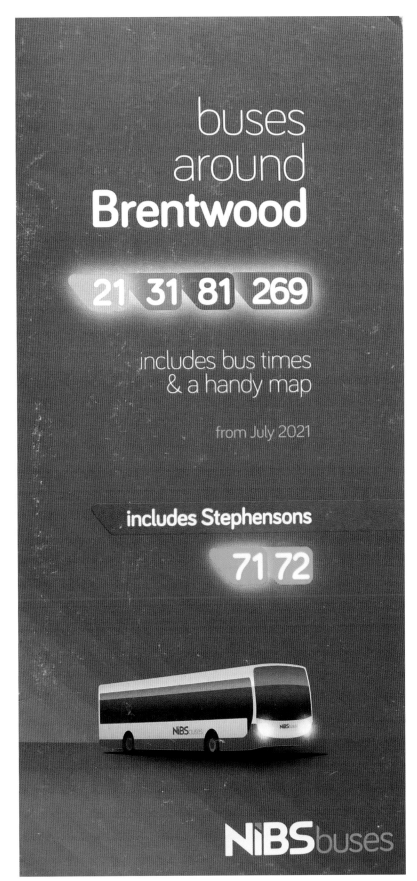

buses
around
Brentwood

21 31 81 269

includes bus times
& a handy map

from July 2021

includes Stephensons

71 72

NiBSbuses

ONGAR

Although a small rural Essex town, Ongar was once served by both London Transport red and green buses and was also the far terminus of the Underground Central Line. The single-line shuttle service from Epping to Ongar closed at the end of September 1994 and has now become the Epping Ongar Railway heritage line. The red buses to Romford ceased in December 1982 when the 247B, by then just three buses a day on market days only, was withdrawn and the nearest that TfL red buses reach now is Passingford Bridge, terminus of the one-bus route 375 from Romford. First Essex, as successors to Eastern National, still work in on weekdays from Chelmsford.

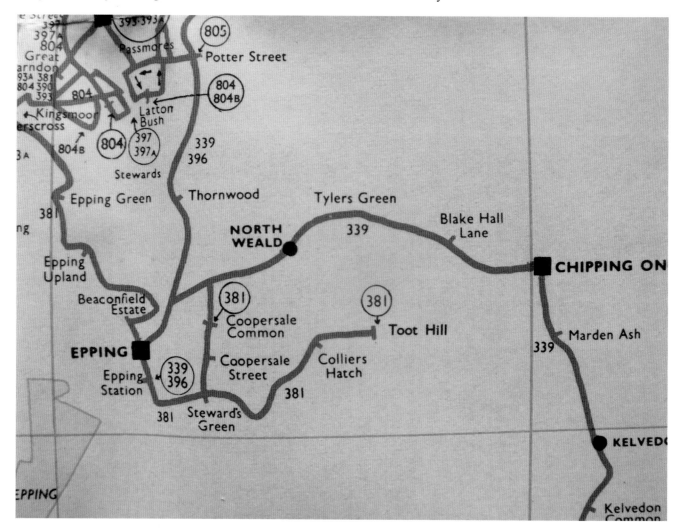

Epping and Ongar area Country Area services 1969.

Recalling the days of London Transport green RTs on the 339, the London Bus Company operates their route 339 on most days when the associated Epping Ongar Railway is operating. Normally two morning and two afternoon journeys run though to Shenfield to bring passengers to and from the station there to the railway. This is the only example of a heritage railway operating their own bus service and the service is also registered to carry normal fare-paying passengers. Green Line liveried RT3228 pauses at the stop for Ongar station in 2018.

Above: On weekdays, a portion of former route 339 runs hourly between Brentwood station and Ongar. Now numbered 21, this was operated by Ensignbus in 2018 but passed to NIBS in 2019. No. 719 was one of many Alexander Dennis E20Ds in the fleet.

Opposite above: The current order on the 21 with NIBS, who have maintained a similar service frequency.

Opposite below: Previously trading as Trustybus, Galleon Travel 2009 Ltd have rebranded their route 420 Harlow–Epping-North Weald-Ongar since 2019 as Central Connect and this has been worked on weekdays by ten former RATP London Scania N230UD double-deck buses.

EPPING

Epping is a busy town and is now the terminus of the Central Line. The line on to Ongar had been reduced to a peak-hours only service from 4 December 1991 and closed at the end of September 1994. As with Brentwood, it was once served by London Transport red and green buses, and also Green Line coaches. The links to Romford have gone and local services to Harlow and Ongar have seen a succession of independent operators since deregulation.

In 1976, London Transport acquired 95 Bristol LHs with ECW bodywork to replace ageing RFs on the more rural services where a 7ft 6in wide vehicle was considered desirable. Romford garage received the first batch for routes 247 to Brentwood and 250 to Epping. BL7 is seen near Epping station on route 247 on 6 July 1979. Routes 247 and 250 had been combined in January 1977 to produce a 25-mile-long Epping–Romford–Brentwood through route.

Above: The 339 originally ran through from Warley (to the south of Brentwood) to Harlow. In London Transport days, RTs would have been used but in May 1978, London Country have put on BN35, a 1974 Bristol LHS6L with just thirty-five seats, seen here having just turned out of Epping station approach.

Below: The local company G.F. Ward of Epping took on route 381 to Coopersale and Toot Hill after withdrawal by LCBS in August 1971. SEV 845K was one of two Ford R192s with Willowbrook DP45F bodies to bus grant standard bought new and is seen near Epping station on 18 May 1978. The other was SOO 223K.

Above: Plymouth Corporation bought a large batch of early Leyland Nationals in 1972 but disposed of them quite early to the benefit of small operators looking for a modern bus. Wards took former Plymouth No. 17 SCO 417L, seen on the 381 on 6 July 1979. It retained Plymouth red livery. A year later, they acquired former London Country RP65. The route passed to Lee-Roy Coaches in 1982.

Opposite above: On 6 July 1979, London Country RP6 stands in Epping High Street on Green Line route 712 to Romford. This route was introduced in May 1978 replacing part of the 703 Bishop's Stortford–Waltham Cross and the Harlow-Romford section of the 724. The 703 had been a part replacement of the 720 London Aldgate–Bishop's Stortford when it was withdrawn in 1977.

Opposite below: Wests Coaches of Woodford Green first got into bus operation when they won the Essex CC tender for route 201 Buckhurst Hill Station to Ongar which had been relinquished by London Buses. Other routes in the Loughton, Chingford and Waltham Cross areas later followed in the 1980s. Following the closure of the Epping–Ongar section of the Central Line in September 1994, they became the replacement operator over this route. This Wright bodied Dennis Dart was new in 1992.

Above: County Bus E564 BNK, a 1988 Volvo B10M with Plaxton Derwent body, was one of a pair acquired from the takeover of Sampsons, Hoddesdon, in 1990. Seen turning from Epping High Street towards the station on 7 May 1996, it carries overall advertising and the local Townlink fleetname. The limited stop 500 was a replacement for the 712. *(M. Batten collection)*

Opposite above: As previously mentioned, by February 1989 the contract for the Sunday service on route 500 Romford-Harlow, which on weekdays was run by London Country (North East), had passed to Blue Triangle. Leyland National TEL 489R loads at Epping station, 30 June 1996.

Opposite below: Locallink was a name used by Stort Valley, Stanstead, for buses operated around Harlow and Bishop's Stortford from December 2001. L901 JRN, an East Lancs bodied Dart formerly with London Central, carries route branding for Bishop's Stortford–Great Dunmow route 319 but was at Epping station on a Sunday tendered working of the 201 to Ongar in June 2003.

Above: Regal Busways' first Essex involvement came in April 2002 with the tendered service 381 Harlow-Toot Hill and routes around Waltham Abbey. This Optare Solo was at the station in 2013.

Opposite above: Centra Passenger Services, the bus division of Central Parking Services, Staines, acquired Locallink in 2004 to add to its rapidly growing business. This Dart was at Epping in June. Within a year, the business had been sold to Rotala and renamed Flights Hallmark. Essex services ended after 27 September and the Sunday 200/201 passed to Regal Busways. Most Centra weekday services went to Trustline/Trustybus.

Opposite below: On 7 February 2011, Arriva ceased running the hourly services 500 Harlow-Epping and 501 Harlow-Ongar on Mondays to Saturdays although it retained a Sunday 501 service. This was due to competition from SM Coaches of Harlow who were now running Monday-Saturday services 19 Harlow-Epping, 20 Harlow-Ongar and 21 Harlow-Brentwood-Warley. SM Coaches EU08 FHC, an Alexander Dennis Enviro200, is on the 19 near Epping station on 17 April 2010. SM Coaches had their licence revoked but rebranded themselves as Townlink in December 2013.

Above: With the opening of the Epping Ongar Railway as a steam and diesel heritage line from 25 May 2012, the London Bus Company began running a connecting service 339 between Epping station and the railway at North Weald at weekends and other days when the railway was operating. Former London Transport vehicles are used and RML900 turns in for the station on 14 April 2018. Some journeys run on to Ongar and from 2014 also to Shenfield as previously seen.

Opposite above: EOS (Swallow Coach Company) started bus operations on 1 September 2014 with route 66 Debden–Harlow (Mon-Sat) and 66A Debden–Upshire (weekdays). X158 FBB was a Plaxton-bodied Volvo B7TL, one of two bought from Go-Ahead London but new to London Easylink. The livery was based on that of Pennine Motor Services from whom they also bought some Dennis Darts.

Route 87 Harlow-Epping was extended from Epping to Loughton in April 2018, replacing the 542 between Loughton and Debden. However, EOS Buses withdrew their routes 66, 86 and 87 from 2 August 2018, earlier than had been notified. Arriva took over from 3 August.

Opposite below: From the end of 26 February 2016, Townlink Buses of Harlow (formerly SM Coaches) had their licences revoked following the third Traffic Commissioners' enquiry since 2011. Services from Harlow to Epping and Ongar were now the preserve of Trustybus, whose routes 419/20 had competed with them since November 2015. In 2018, the route was mostly worked by these Scania OmniCity buses. The service ran up to a fifteen-minute frequency between Epping and Harlow on Monday–Friday peak hours as many commuters from the Harlow area prefer to use Epping as it is the start of the (very frequent) Central line and so they can expect to get a seat on the train.

Above: Yes, this is Epping in 2019, despite the bus claiming to be from West Yorkshire! Galleon Travel (Trustybus) bought this Scania OmniCity 'which was new to Nottingham City Transport' from Harrogate-based company Connexions Buses. They had repainted it in the National Bus Company poppy red livery of West Yorkshire who used to serve Harrogate. The new owners ran the bus in 'as acquired' livery and blinds had not yet been fitted.

Below: By 2019, the Arriva services in Essex and Hertfordshire were operated under the Arriva Kent Thameside licence. This long Optare Solo from Harlow was seen at Epping and as shown on the digital blind display will travel as far south as Loughton on former EOS service 87, a place still served by TfL red buses.

HARLOW

Harlow was a new town, planned and constructed from 1948 onwards to take London's overspill population after the devastation caused by bombing during wartime.

It has probably had more changes to its bus network since 1970 than any of the other towns featured in this book. Only a brief selection can be included here. Full details of the route and operator changes can be found in *London Bus Magazine,* the newsletter of the London Omnibus Traction Society, and from 2001 on the Harlowride website www.harlowride.co.uk.

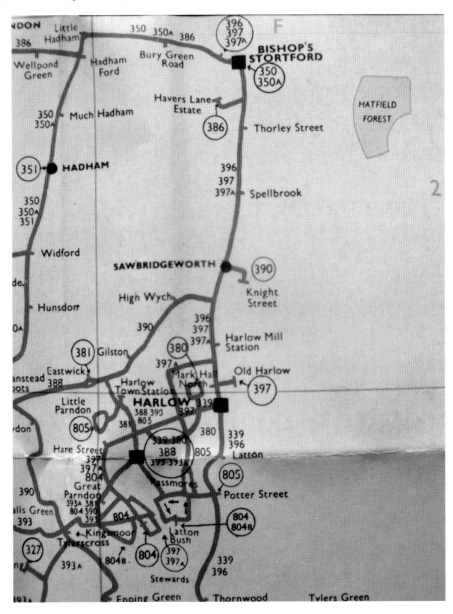

Harlow and Bishop's Stortford area Country Area services 1969.

Above: London Country Bus Services started a Dial-a-Bus type operation in Harlow in August 1974, where passengers could book a bus by phone which would call as near to their front door as possible at a lower fare than a taxi. Marketed as Pick-me-Up, Ford Transits with Dormobile 16 seat bodies were the vehicles of choice. FT5 stands in the bus station on 16 October. Unfortunately, the high costs of operation with drivers on big bus wages and the need for dispatchers made it uneconomical.

Opposite above: In 1976, London Country was suffering from a severe shortage of serviceable buses and hired in vehicles from various municipal fleets. Harlow garage received some Leyland PD3/6 buses from Southend with Massey H38/32R bodywork which were used on route 339. CJN 441C was at the garage on 28 April. These buses had earlier been hired by London Transport and used out of Croydon garage – note the LT style garage code HA for Harlow and running number plate below the front nearside window.

Opposite below: On the same day, at the bus station is Eastern National 1436. This is a 1962 Bristol MW6G coach, downgraded and fitted with bus seats. Note the registration OO 9544. This unusual occurrence of a two-letter registration on a vehicle this late was because OO and WC were two previously unused sequences that were allocated to Essex in 1961. WC was only used with a prefix letter (e.g. BWC) though. This bus was allocated to Bishop's Stortford (BS).

Above: In 1986, London Buses introduced commercial route X99 from Harlow to Basildon, hourly Monday–Saturday marketed as 'The Forester'. Leyland Nationals were used, reseated with coach seats and painted in this dedicated livery. LS27 is arriving at Harlow on the first day, 2 August, when no fares were charged, hence the very full bus! The route only lasted for six months. (*M. Batten collection*)

Left and opposite above: A publicity leaflet for the X99, showing the route taken by the service.

Opposite below: A line-up of London Country (North East) Atlanteans at Harlow garage on 7 August 1988. Some are in the new livery then being introduced. Following the MAP analysis, a new network "Townbus' with 'T' routes' came in from 30 August 1980.

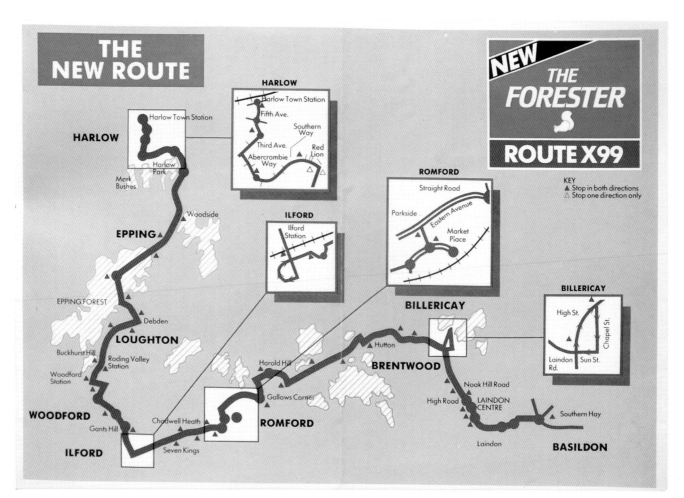

Above: On the same day, London Country (North East) TP70 stands in the bus station on Green Line route 724 to Heathrow Airport. London Country had started to upgrade Green Line services with coaches in 1977 and this is a 1984 Leyland Tiger with Plaxton C49F bodywork.

Opposite above: Before the Sunday tendered service on route 500 Romford–Harlow passed to Blue Triangle in February 1989 (see p 43), it had been worked by London Buses in 1988. So here we have the unusual sight of a red London bus at Harlow. LS 235 was arriving on 7 August.

Opposite below: In 1988-9, Essex County Council funded a Sunday leisure bus service 622 every two hours from Harlow to Great Yeldham, taking in a number of tourist attraction villages such as Dunmow, plus Castle Hedingham and the Colne Valley Railway. Blue Triangle had the contract which specified vintage vehicles, and normally used ex-London Transport RTs. Weymann bodied RT2799 was also taken on 7 August 1988.

Above: London Country (North East) was split into County Bus serving Essex and Sovereign Bus serving Hertfordshire in January 1989. Local area brandings were adopted, and the Harlow buses became Townlink. Leyland Olympian LR58 with Roe bodywork sports the brand lettering on the LCNE livery as it waits for custom at Harlow Town station on 26 June 1989.

Opposite above: Golden Boy, Roydon, are a long-established coach operator. They also ran stage services for a while after deregulation. FCY 283W was a 1980 Bedford YMQ with Duple DP45F body which had been acquired from Armchair, Bedford. It had been new to South Wales as No. 280. This was at Harlow bus station on 26 June 1989.

Opposite below: The first new company to compete on Harlow town services was Buzz Co-operative. This was set up by seven ex-London Country (North East) drivers in October 1988. Initially, seven services were registered, running twelve hours a day Monday-Saturday with frequencies varying between 10min and 30min. Nine Mercedes-Benz 609Ds were bought at first. F365 BUA was one of two new Optare StarRiders when seen on 26 June 1989. Competition ended in 1990 with Buzz retaining Monday-Saturday routes B1 and B6 and peak-hours B11, the other routes being withdrawn.

Above: County Bus Volkswagen LT55 City Pacer E520 PWR on a local service to Old Harlow in 1992. These vehicles, MB806-20, were acquired with the takeover of Welwyn-Hatfield Line in 1991.

Opposite above: Red London buses returned to Harlow in 1996 when MTL London, who had bought the London Northern unit of London Buses in 1994, started route 310B from Enfield Town to Harlow. There was also a 310A to Hertford competing with the LCBS route 310. This 'one-off' DAF SB220/Ikarus was at Enfield on 13 April 1996. The 310B had ceased by 1998 although the 310A carried on longer. The buses operated from Potters Bar garage.

Opposite below: A newcomer to Essex in September 2000 was Imperial Bus Company of Rainham with a half-hourly Monday-Saturday route 100 between Loughton and Buckhurst Hill stations via Debden, competing with parts of TfL's routes 20 and 167. Imperial introduced commercial Monday-Friday route H1 between Harlow and Loughton in September 2001. Former LT Leyland Titan T379 sets out from Harlow on 3 April 2002. It was extended to Buckhurst Hill Station in March 2003 but cut back again in November.

Above: County Bus had passed with Cowie Group ownership to become Arriva East Herts & Essex. New at Harlow in late 1999 were eight Volvo B6BLEs with Wright bodywork branded for routes 500/2. The 500, run on a London Local Service Agreement, was withdrawn between Ongar and Romford from 6 July 2008 as a result of the introduction of the Low Emission Zone from the following day.

Below: SM Travel started in the 1990s. L657 MFL was one of three Volvo B6/Marshall B32F buses that originated with Cambus at Cambridge. Taken on 7 May 2003.

Above: Olympian Coaches started off as an offshoot of SM Travel but developed into a separate operation. In 2003, their fleet was mostly Mercedes-Benz minibuses but did include this one early Dennis Dart with Carlyle bodywork, also seen on 7 May 2003. A directive from the 2012 London Olympics authority required them to change their name and in 2006 they split into two licences, Olympus Bus & Coach Ltd and Roadrunner Coaches Ltd.

Below: Locallink, Bishop's Stortford CWR 522Y, a Leyland Olympian/ECW originally with Yorkshire Woollen District, is seen here on 7 May 2003. It had come from UK North, whose livery and name it was still carrying. After Locallink were taken over by Centra, the 410 route and other services ended in 2004.

Above: On 5 January 2008, Trustline began a Monday-Saturday daytime circular service 22/23 every fifteen minutes competing with similar Arriva route 2/3 between Harlow Town station and Staple Tye. They used former ChesterBus Dennis Darts. One of these, L63 SFM, is seen later in September 2008 carrying the Trustybus fleetname which replaced Trustline that year.

Opposite above: Unusual vehicles for SM Coaches of Harlow were three of these Irisbus Daily low-floor buses with Unvi LoGo bodywork in 2007.

Opposite below: Green Line route 724 from Harlow-Heathrow Airport still remains but not now with coaches. In 2006, nine Mercedes-Benz Citaros took over, albeit in Green Line livery. Funding for these was helped by a quality partnership with Hertfordshire CC and BAA Heathrow. To improve timetable reliability, some sections of the route prone to delays were bypassed and nineteen of the seventy stops removed. BU06 HSD reaches journey's end at Harlow and waits to turn in for the bus station on 27 September 2008. By 2017 they had received Arriva fleet livery with only a nominal reference to the Green Line branding.

Above: Yet more competition came to the Harlow area in 2008 when TWH (Travel With Hunny) started weekday hourly service 55 to Loughton. This competed with Imperial's service. Two Scania L113CRL buses ex-Stagecoach Yorkshire were used. Alexander-bodied M953 DRG is seen at the Loughton end of the route on 24 October 2008. Later in the year they also offered an L55 Christmas shoppers' link extended to Lakeside shopping centre. From 1 September 2009, they gained a contract for route 392 Harlow-Rye Park, formerly with Stanstead Transit and then Excel.

Opposite above: Roadrunner, Harlow, was associated with SM Travel, also of Harlow, although their operations were separated in 2010. Acquired that year were former Transdev London Volvo B7TL/ Plaxton W461/2/8/73 BCW.

Opposite below: In 2010, Arriva, as successors to County Bus, transferred the Harlow services from its Shires & Essex subsidiary to its wholly-owned TGM Group subsidiary. They merged this with the Excel services at Stanstead which they had taken over in 2008. A new Network Harlow brand identity was created with route 1 relaunched as Red Route 1 in August with these Dennis Dart SLF/Wright Crusader buses. The Network Harlow identity was dropped in 2015 when Harlow operations ceased being part of Arriva TGM Group and were placed back under Arriva Southern Counties.

Above: Roadrunner competed with Centrebus between Harlow and Waltham Cross, mainly using these sixteen-year-old Scania N113CRL/Wright buses new to London Buses and more recently with Your Bus in Nottingham. Also taken on 21 September 2010.

Opposite above: A TGM Essex Optare Solo. These were all repainted in this two-tone blue livery and Network Harlow branding from 2011.

Opposite below: A new venture from 4 June 2018 saw EOS launch express service S1 from Harlow to Stratford via the M11 motorway. Running Mondays-Fridays approximately every two hours, it stopped at only Redbridge station and Stratford City bus station in London. On 29 June, the 15.30 departure leaves Stratford and passes by the International Station on its way back to Harlow. The regular vehicle was ex-Go-Ahead London ED27, an MCV bodied Alexander Dennis Enviro200 still in LT red livery. However, the route was withdrawn at the end of July without replacement.

BISHOP'S STORTFORD

Bishop's Stortford has become more important with the development of the nearby Stanstead Airport as London's third airport from 1979. A rail link to Stanstead Airport opened in 1991 with a Stanstead Express service from London Liverpool Street. National Express launched a packet of services to the airport from April 1992 including an hourly service from London Victoria calling at Aldgate, Stratford and Wanstead stations and with a journey time of 80 minutes. By 2015, the airport had become the third busiest in the UK and now has frequent National Express services to Stratford and London.

Above: London Transport and later London Country Green Line route 720 ran from London to Bishop's Stortford via Harlow. An extension was made to Stanstead Airport in May 1974, but this was in the era before cheap flights – the traffic wasn't forthcoming and the whole route was withdrawn after 1 April 1977. It was replaced by the 702 from Walthamstow to Bishop's Stortford but this in turn became bus route 502 from 12 May 1984. London Country RF39, a former Green Line vehicle now in the yellow and green bus livery, waits at Aldgate bus station on 29 March 1974.

Opposite above: In 1974-5, the NBC ordered lightweight Bedford or Ford chassis for many of their fleets as a quicker delivery alternative to the Bristol LH which was the standard smaller bus than the Leyland National. Eastern National received 1000-4 MAR 775-9P, Ford R1014s with Duple B43F bodies in 1976. No. 1003 is seen outside the Bishop's Stortford garage on 28 April where they were all based.

Below: Biss Bros, Bishop's Stortford, had some local routes. 1966 Bedford SB5/Duple Midland HJU 339D is going to that well-known location 'Service' – hopefully the passengers know better. 25 May 1978.

Above: In 1986, a rail-air bus link from Bishop's Stortford was provided by Eastern National. Leyland Tiger/Alexander C53F No. 1111 carries the special livery for this and was an exhibit at the 1986 Showbus Rally held at Woburn. This would have ceased when the rail link to Stanstead Airport opened in 1991.

Below: After Drawlane bought London Country (South West) in 1988, they set up a new company 'Speedlink Airport Services' to work the airport services that had been developed under the Green Line brand. Jetlink 747 had started non-stop between Gatwick and Heathrow in 1979, later extended to Luton via Watford in 1986. From 12 April 1992, the route was extended every two hours on to Stevenage, Bishop's Stortford and Stanstead Airport, thus linking all London's airports. This Plaxton-bodied Leyland Tiger is lettered for the extension at Heathrow in March 1994.

Above: Excel, Stanstead, was an offshoot of Stephensons of Rochford, Essex. They started in July 2003 after First Essex closed down much of their operations in Bishop's Stortford. They had three ex-Stagecoach Mercedes-Benz 709D/Alexander minibuses in this livery for town services 308-9 when this was taken in August 2003. Excel was purchased by Tellings-Golden Miller (TGM) in 2008, who were by then a wholly-owned Arriva subsidiary.

Below: A route-branded version of Arriva corporate livery for route 510 Harlow–Bishop's Stortford–Stanstead Airport, again in August 2003. This was a DAF SB220 with Optare Delta bodywork.

Above: More route branding but on a special livery for First Essex 430, a Mercedes-Benz 0814.

Below: Richmond's, Royston remained in operation in 2022 with a number of local routes. At Bishop's Stortford in 2003 was this Optare Solo.

STEVENAGE & HITCHIN

Stevenage was the first designated 'new town'. It was also where the new LCBS company would first make major changes to local services.

Superbus was a concept introduced in 1971 following a Department of the Environment report in 1969 suggesting that the transport needs of the town could be met by high quality bus services rather than further road building. Between 26 October and 7 November 1970, residents were invited to take a free ride on a pair

of modern single-deck buses and complete a short questionnaire about their features. The vehicles used were a pair of new LCBS AEC Swifts SM146-7 and two Metro-Scanias – the demonstrator VWD 451H which had earlier been trialled by London Transport, and Leicester City Transport No. 136, WOE 488J. This led to the farebox-equipped Swifts replacing ex-London Transport RT type double-deckers on route 809 to Chells in May 1971 and then the Superbus route SB1 from July.

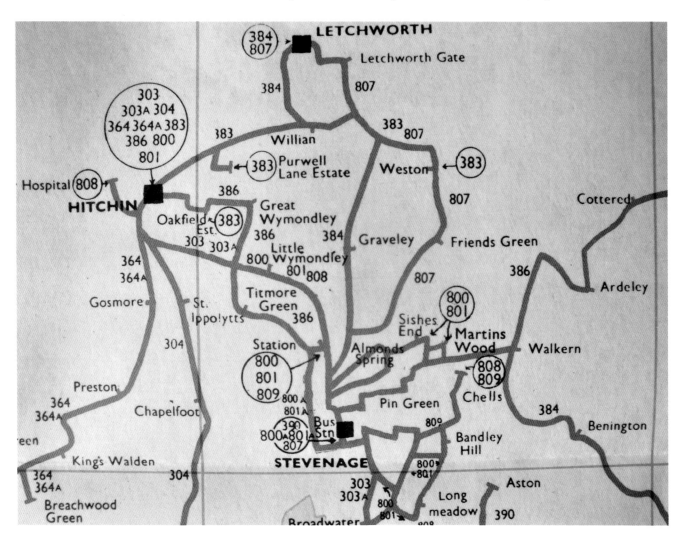

Stevenage and Hitchin area Country Area services 1969.

Three days before LCBS started, London Transport had also started the Blue Arrow service with three XF class Daimler Fleetlines. This was a service to industrial estates timed around company start/finish times, stopping wherever convenient rather than at fixed stops, and with pre-booked season tickets only available.

After being the last National Bus Company to be privatised in April 1988, London Country (North East) got off to a bad start with a ten-day strike. Hertfordshire County Council said that it had received more than 330 complaints about cancellations, early and late running and rudeness. The company had £116,000 in revenue support withheld for not running tendered services, with a further £43,000 levied but suspended pending their putting their house in order. There was a six-month ban on introducing new services other than planned minibus routes in St. Albans.

London Country inherited an ageing fleet with few double-deck vehicles suitable for one-person operation. An early purchase was of ninety Leyland Atlanteans with Park Royal bodies. AN65 loads at Stevenage bus station on local service 801. London Transport used country route numbers in the 300 series north of the Thames and 400 series south of the Thames but had exhausted the range when the new towns of Harlow and Stevenage were built, so the new local bus routes took 800 series numbers (500s/600s being trolleybus routes and 700s Green Line). Note the sign stating an exact fare of 8p. 10 September 1974.

Above: The first flat-fare route SB1 replaced route 809 to Chells on 31 July 1971. Five of the 1970 built AEC Swifts were painted in a blue and yellow livery and SM497 is seen also on 10 September 1974.

Below: The AEC Swifts ran in comparison trials with four Metro-Scanias and from 1972 also four early Leyland Nationals. In 1973, LCBS gained three more Metro-Scanias. These had been acquired by fellow NBC fleet Hants & Dorset with the takeover of Winchester based company King Alfred Motor Services. They were exchanged with LCBS for three Leyland Nationals. Former King Alfred AOU 110J is at Stevenage on 28 April 1976.

Above: London Country Atlantean AN40 on route SB1 displays the 'Stevenage Bus' branding that replaced Superbus in 1980 under the NBC's MAP scheme. The bus station dates from 1958 and was replaced by an interchange near the railway station in 2022. 14 June 1980.

Below: On 12 October 1985, Simmonds Coaches of Letchworth were using this Plaxton bodied Leyland Leopard coach on former LCBS route 382.

Above: Charles Cook of Biggleswade operated a route between their hometown and Stevenage via Stotfold and Baldock. Vehicles operated included ex-London Transport Daimler Fleetline DMS439 and former MD18, a Scania BR111DH/MCW Metropolitan, acquired in 1984. This also taken on 12 October 1985.

Below: Jubilee Coaches of Stevenage dated back to 1969 but had been bought by Contractus Ltd in 1980 and operated under that name until 1983. They won two Stevenage town services on Hertfordshire contracts in 1986. This scruffy and battered ex-London Fleetline, once DMS 392, is not the best advertisement for the company. A paper label in the windscreen gives the destination details '387 Bus station–Bragbury End' while the other label above the windscreen says, 'Hertfordshire County Council contract bus service'. 11 March 1987.

Above: Hitchin was on the border and was also United Counties territory – they had a garage there. Their route 314 penetrated the LCBS territory as far south as Welwyn Garden City where Bristol VR No. 582 is heading for Hitchin on 11 March 1987. Note the Hertfordshire CC contract sign in the windscreen.

Opposite above: Under new ownership, Jubilee Coaches started six commercial minibus services in February 1988 with leased MCW Metroriders. The routes were marketed as Road Hopper. Some traversed previously unserved roads but elsewhere they were in competition with LCNE. They bought or leased several new vehicles, and this is a 1988 Leyland Lynx. When photographed on 3 June 1989 it was actually owned by Sovereign Bus & Coach. This was the name for the northern and western part of London Country (North East) serving Stevenage, St. Albans, etc. after the company had been split in two in January 1989. They had then acquired Jubilee Coaches later that month, January 1989.

Opposite below: A Sovereign MCW Metrorider in 1990. They adopted this blue/white livery and HERTSrider name.

Above: Luton & District took four Leyland Swifts with Wadham Stringer B35F bodies in 1989. They were allocated to Hitchin for tendered routes including the 384 (Stevenage–Hertford via Walkern) which had previously been worked by London Country (North East) and briefly by Jubilee Coaches.

Below: On 20 May 1990 Luton & District took over a large part of Sovereign Bus & Coach's Stevenage operations, including some town services, route 301 Stevenage–Hitchin, coach services 750 Hemel Hempstead–Ware and 797 Cambridge–London. Forty-two vehicles were transferred with buses given the Stevenage Bus branding as on former London Country Leyland National No. 441 on 20 August 1990.

Above: On the same day, this Green Line liveried Duple C53F bodied Leyland Tiger, formerly London Country and Sovereign TDL51, has now become Luton & District 121. This is on route 797 Cambridge–Stevenage–London which was transferred in the May takeover.

Below: Chambers, Stevenage, were running the 382 route in August 1990 when this Leyland Swift/Wadham Stringer bus was seen.

Above: Luton & District used the 'Hoppanstopper' brand for their minibuses. This Iveco 49-10 was on route 400 to Hitchin in 1991.

Opposite above: In 1993, Sovereign Leyland National JUB 642V takes on passengers for Chells on local service SB11. On 17 March 1996, local services to Symonds Green, Poplars and Shephall passed to the Shires (formerly Luton & District) leaving Sovereign with only the Chells route. However, Sovereign took back the Green Line 797. This was still running and profitably so in 2004, although now just Baldock-Stevenage-London.

Opposite below: The University of Hertfordshire started a commercial venture 'Universitybus' in 1992 to carry students to their campuses at Hatfield and Wall Hall, Aldenham and nurses to various hospitals as the local bus services were seen as inadequate. The general public were also conveyed as a way of raising revenue. By 1993, routes ran from St. Albans-Hatfield, Welwyn–Watford, and Watford–Hitchin, competing in places against Sovereign Bus & Coach. Universitybus were early users of the American Blue Bird buses when these were marketed in the UK and one of their four is departing Stevenage on the then irregular route 634 for Watford in 1995.

Above: Blazefield Holdings, owners of Sovereign Bus, ran down some of their southern operations in the early 2000s to concentrate on their main businesses in Lancashire and Yorkshire. The St. Albans area was sold to Centrebus in 2003, a company based in, and mainly running in, Leicestershire. That left Sovereign with just the Stevenage and Hatfield garages in Hertfordshire. The Hatfield garage was new in January 2003, jointly shared with Universitybus. The remaining part of Sovereign was proposed for sale to Arriva in 2004, thus bringing all of the former parts of LCBS into Arriva. The Office of Fair Trading requested a report into this by the Competitions Commission, but they cleared the takeover which took place on 23 January 2005. From 1 January 2015, Stevenage, along with Hemel Hempstead and Ware, became part of Arriva Southern Counties. This is a Wright-bodied Volvo B10BLE in 2002. Note the revival of the 'SB' branding first used in the 1970s.

Opposite above: Stanstead Transit – under the Transit Group Ltd licence – started Stevenage town services in 2004, competing against Arriva. From 10 November, they registered circular route X1 to Chells on weekdays, every five minutes. These two Dennis Darts were displayed at Showbus, Duxford Airfield in September 2004.

Opposite below: Trustline (Galleon Travel) took over express route 700 from Stevenage to Stanstead Airport from Arriva in March 2006 and bought two Alexander Dennis Darts with MCV Evolution bodywork as seen running in June 2007. By 2015, this route was with Centrebus.

Universitybus rebranded themselves as Uno in 2004 with an unusual pink/mauve livery by Best Impressions. By now they had become the second largest operator in Hertfordshire after Arriva, operating fifty vehicles and carrying more than 2.5 million passengers a year. However, market research had shown that one third of bus users in the county did not realise that the services were available to the general public as well as students, hence the new approach. Scania YN56 NRZ departs from Stevenage in June 2007 again on the 634, which was revamped in 2004 as an hourly express between Stevenage and Hemel Hempstead using the M10 and A1(M) motorways. Uno also expanded by taking over the St. Albans local services from Centrebus in 2008.

Stevenage finally lost its Green Line service when the 797, by then just Stevenage–London and worked by Arriva, was withdrawn at the end of February 2015. Uno put on a replacement service 797 using Mercedes-Benz Citaros in Green Line livery. But after six months it was cut back to Baker Street to improve reliability and reduce the number of buses required; and then in March 2016 the hourly service was reduced to a single peak-hour journey which only lasted to 2 September.

LUTON

The Bedfordshire town of Luton was the only location on the borders of London Transport's country area with a municipally owned fleet. Here LT buses were not allowed to carry local passengers. The town was also served by United Counties who had a garage there. However, on 4 January 1970 the loss-making Corporation fleet sold out to United Counties, who were by now part of the National Bus Company, for £294,824.

United Counties had operated buses in Luton from 1952. Prior to this, it had been the Midland Area of Eastern National. United Counties would be split up three ways from 1 January 1986. The Luton and Aylesbury area became Luton & District with 166 buses, 21 coaches, and garages at Luton, Leighton Buzzard, Hitchin and Aylesbury. Milton Keynes local services became Milton Keynes City Bus while the rest remained as United Counties. The Luton & District fleet was privatised when it was sold to its employees on 21 August 1987. By then it operated 260 buses, including 73 minibuses.

A service X5 to Milton Keynes was introduced by Luton & District at deregulation.

Luton also has an airport. Since 1999 this has had a separate station, Luton Airport Parkway, but prior to that there were buses run from the main station on behalf of airlines. In 1980, following the deregulation of express services over thirty miles, LCBS introduced a new Green Line service '757' from Luton Airport and Luton to London Victoria. This initially ran hourly on weekdays via the M1 motorway and competed with a service by Seamarks Coaches. In June 1988, Luton & District took over sole responsibility for the 757, which had been jointly operated with London Country (North East) since February. The 757 developed into a highly successful service running up to every fifteen minutes but in May 2013 it was evicted from the airport when Luton Airport signed a deal with National Express to provide a faster and more frequent service 'A1' to London. Fortunately for

Arriva, the eviction was overturned from March 2014 when a High Court judgement found that the airport's actions were an abuse of the Competition Act.

In September 2013, a 7.7mile guided busway opened between Luton and the nearby town of Dunstable, over the route of a disused railway, closed to passengers in 1965 but retained for freight to the 1980s. This had been proposed in 1991 because of severe congestion on the roads. In 2008, nearly five years after the Department for Transport had granted outline approval, it gave Luton Borough Council the permission to seek tenders to build the busway at a then estimated cost of £84.4m of which the DfT would provide £78.4m. Changes to the structure of local government – Luton became a unitary authority in 1997 and Bedfordshire was abolished and replaced in this area by the Central Bedfordshire Council in 2009 – meant that funding was only finally confirmed in 2010 and construction could start. It opened on 25 September 2013, eventually costing £91m and becoming the UK's second longest guided busway. By this time, the population of the area served was 257,000 of which 205,000 were in Luton, 35,000 in Dunstable and 17,000 in Houghton Regis – a former village that had developed as a London overspill location. The busway has been served by three bus companies – Arriva, Centrebus and Grant Palmer.

A 2008 business case anticipated 9,000 trips a day on the busway but results for the first three months showed only 41 per cent of expected usage with just under 350,000 passengers carried. The councils were considering adding two additional stops and blamed the economic downturn. Passenger levels have picked up since then. Arriva added another route 'Z' in 2015 which replaced parts of existing routes 38/39. Arriva also operate interurban routes F70 and F77 to Milton Keynes and Bletchley which use the busway. By mid-2018, the Luton end had over twenty buses an hour using it.

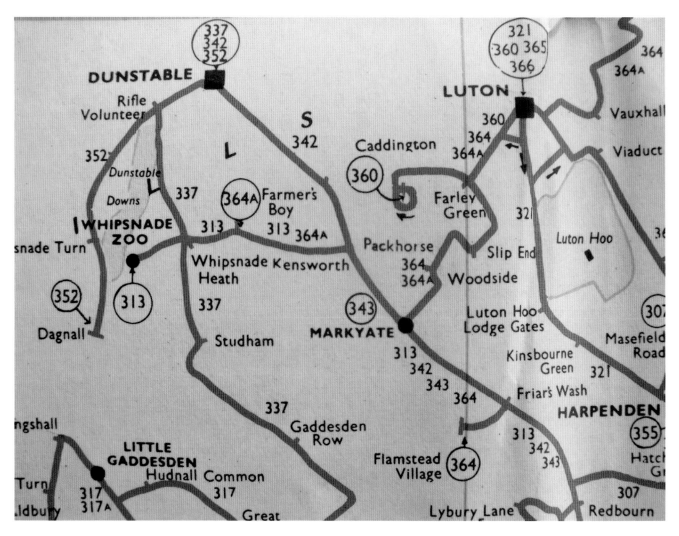

Above: Luton area Country Area services 1969.

Left: Luton Corporation tickets.

Above: Luton Corporation 153, a 1959 Leyland PD2/30 with Weymann lowbridge bodywork, is at the bus station in front of the central library on 6 August 1969.

Below: Leyland buses had predominated in the Luton fleet, but in 1965 they bought 181-6 Dennis Loline IIIs with Neepsend H39/30F bodies. They had earlier bought two Loline IIs in 1960.

Above: From 1967, Luton turned to the Bristol RE which had just become available on the open market rather than just restricted to nationalised companies. A total of thirty were bought with ECW B48D bodies and 119 dates from 1969.

Opposite above: Luton Corporation sold out to neighbours United Counties on 4 January 1970. They quickly repainted most of the seventy-seven buses acquired but being non-standard in their fleet, the double-deckers were soon replaced and sold. This is 1963 Albion Lowlander 171 now as United Counties 831 on 19 April 1970. The Bristol REs however were retained as of course they were a standard type in their fleet. Five Bristol LHS buses on order were transferred to Eastern Counties and re-registered.

Opposite below: Typical of the United Counties fleet at the time, 1954 Bristol LS6G 478, originally Red & White U454, at Luton bus station on 6 August 1969. Buses reversed into the stands as most double-deck buses had rear entrances.

Above: London Country Leyland National SNB204 lays over before working a journey on route 360 to Caddington in 1977. Presumably it will not start from the bus stop seen, as the bus is on the wrong side of the road. LCBS reduced services in the area and closed their Luton garage on 28 January 1977, the first of their garages to close. Routes 360 and 365 passed to United Counties in December 1976. (*M. Batten collection*)

Opposite above: Luton Airport was served by Green Line routes 707 and 717 from January 1977. But an express service via the M1 motorway had to wait until the 1980 deregulation when, from 1 November, the hourly Monday-Saturday 757 began from London Victoria. The service rapidly grew, doubling in frequency and adding a Sunday service in 1982 and a new name – Flightline 757. This was one of the first routes to receive the new TL class ECW-bodied Leyland Tigers and TL3 is seen at Victoria when new in 1982.

Opposite below: The southern part of United Counties was hived off as Luton & District in January 1986. A new red and white livery was adopted with local area fleetnames. Now sporting a 'Luton Bus' name is former United Counties 780, a 1972 Bristol VR/ECW, on 28 May 1988.

Above: The independent Red Rover company of Aylesbury (see p. 137) was taken over by Luton & District in January 1988. This is one of three former South Yorkshire PTE Leyland Fleetlines with London DMS style MCW bodies that were acquired by Red Rover in 1977 and passed to Luton & District. Working former Red Rover route 61 and retaining Red Rover colours, it carries both its old number (166) and new number (704) on 28 May 1988.

Opposite above: Luton Airport lies to the south of town and did not have a station until Luton Airport Parkway opened in 1999. Connecting buses ran from the main station and Luton & District Leyland National 477 is on the Luton Flyer rail-air link. 28 May 1988.

Opposite below: Buffalo Bus came from Flitwick, north of Luton. F154 KGS is a 1988 Leyland Swift with Wadham Stringer B39F body bought new. This was arriving at Luton bus station on 3 July 1989. This bus station by the station and under cover had replaced the earlier location by the library in 1976.

Above: After deregulation in 1986, evening and Sunday services on routes which were otherwise registered as commercial were often not considered as commercially profitable and would be put out to tender. Thus, these services were often awarded to different operators whose wage rates might be lower and so could put in a lower bid. The trunk former London Transport/London Country route 321 (Luton–Watford–Maple Cross) was one such route and the tender went to Seamarks of Luton. In 1989 they bought two DAF SB220/Optare buses for their routes. A further vehicle added later was G971 TTM, seen here in St. Albans in July 1990.

Opposite above: A fleet of thirty-seven Freight Rover Sherpa minibuses entered service with Luton & District from 18 July 1987 under the 'Hoppanstopper' brand in this attractive livery scheme. Luton had four services during weekdays, two every 12 minutes, two every 30 minutes. Dunstable had four routes every 6 minutes from 06.00-18.45 and every 20 minutes thereafter. Two routes linked the two towns every 10 minutes.

Opposite below: Competition came from Lutonian starting in 1984, even before deregulation. This 1988 Freight Rover Sherpa seen in 1992 had bodywork by Aitken of Linlithgow and came from Inverness Traction after that company was taken over by Stagecoach and their fleet replaced. Lutonian remained independent until 1998, when Arriva the Shires, as successor to Luton & District, took them over. However, the Monopolies and Mergers Commission decided that the acquisition was down to unfair competitive tactics and ordered Arriva to sell off Lutonian, which happened in September 2000.

Above: In a new initiative, believed to be a UK first, Luton & District created a fleet of ten Bristol VRs as dedicated school buses from the start of the autumn term 1988. They operated school services around Luton and Dunstable in a distinctive livery. Buses and drivers normally stayed on the same run to create a local sense of belonging with the pupils. However, in 1995 they were also used on ordinary bus routes 27 and 31 as here on 4 July 1995.

Opposite above: From November 1988, Luton & District took delivery of twelve Leyland Olympians with Alexander bodies. They were all initially allocated to Luton for routes 37/38 between Stopsley or Luton Airport to Dunstable via Houghton Regis. However, No. 640 is seen at Watford Junction station in March 1993 on the former London Transport/London Country route 321 to Luton. In 1992 this had become the first bus repainted in red and cream, matching the style of the green/grey livery used on the former London Country (North West) vehicles as seen on the bus behind.

Opposite below: In 1992, the Sunday tendered service on route 321 was won by Capital Citybus. Leyland Olympian No. 156 stands at Rickmansworth. A typical full London Transport style blind display is provided with a range of intermediate points served. Contrast this with the display on the Luton & District Olympian in the previous photograph.

Above: New competition came to Luton from 25 November 1991 when the aptly named Challenger Travel began running. Freight Rover Sherpas ex-Bee Line Buzz were used such as D213 OOJ working route C25 in competition to Luton & District route 25. British Bus, then owners of Luton & District, reached agreement with Challenger which led to their ceasing operations in July 1994.

Opposite above: Luton & District introduced a new blue and yellow livery designed by Best Impressions in 1995 which would replace the red / cream Luton area and green / grey London Country area liveries. As the company now operated in areas well away from Luton, the company name was changed to The Shires following a competition amongst employees, and local fleetnames were applied for each area served. Carrying the new livery and Luton & Dunstable name in 1996 is 33, a Mercedes-Benz 811D with Wadham Stringer bodywork. This was one of twenty originally bought by Bournemouth in 1989 but soon sold on after public criticism. This one was bought by Buffalo Travel, Flitwick and passed on to The Shires in 1995 (see below). The others all went to Brighton & Hove.

Opposite below: The bus services of Buffalo Travel, Flitwick, were acquired by The Shires (formerly Luton & District) on 22 May 1995 along with 24 vehicles. This brought The Shires into new territory such as Bedford and Milton Keynes. Former Nottingham Leyland Olympian A698 EAU was one of the vehicles that would pass to The Shires and is seen on the Milton Keynes route in 1992.

Above: Luton Airport bought at least three of these DAF SB220/Ikarus buses in 1996. Taken outside Luton station, M832 RCP carries branding for Monarch Airlines.

Opposite above: The Shires introduced the concept of 'Sapphire' routes to Luton in November 1995 with services 31/X31 to Dunstable and Leighton Buzzard. Vehicles and drivers were dedicated to these services. New Scania L113CRL/East Lancs B51F buses were supplied for the 31 and refurbished Olympians for the X31. A well-loaded N699 EUR was photographed when new on 1 June 1996. A second scheme on routes 24/25/26 with new Volvo Olympians followed later in the year.

Opposite below: The first low-floor double-deckers in the former Country Area came to Luton in July 2000 with twelve Dennis Tridents for route 38 to Dunstable, which saw off the last Bristol VRs from the fleet. In 2000 although Arriva kept the former Luton & District and County Bus operations as separate entities (although under common management), they changed the 'descriptor' strapline to 'serving the Shires and Essex'.

Above: Lutonian Buses had started up again in 2000 after Arriva were ordered to sell it off. The company with twenty-four buses was bought by Leicester-based Centrebus on 18 June 2004. This Wright-bodied Dennis Dart ex-Go North East was on the Marsh Farm service in June 2003.

Opposite above: Arriva the Shires introduced seven liquefied natural gas-powered DAF SB220 buses on to route 321 in November 1999. The route was extended back to its original London Transport terminus at Rickmansworth in 2000, which prompted the transfer of other LPG powered DAFs from elsewhere within the Arriva empire. No. 4422, seen in Watford High Street in 2004, came from Arriva Cymru. These buses were converted to diesel by 2006. Mercedes-Benz Citaros took over the 321 in 2008 until they were in turn replaced by Wright Streetlites in 2014, fitted out and liveried in the premium 'Sapphire' branding.

Opposite below: EasyBus, a low-fare minibus subsidiary of Easy Jet, started a competing service from London to Luton Airport with van-conversion Mercedes-Benz Sprinters. In 2007 they started services to Stanstead and Gatwick airports, but the Luton service was incorporated into Arriva's Green Line 757 route. Arriva painted four of their DAF SB3000/Plaxton coaches into the easyBus orange livery. No. 4054 was on the stand at Buckingham Place Road, London on 22 May 2007.

Above: One of eleven Volvo B7RLEs with Wright bodywork bought by Arriva the Shires, originally for route 38 Luton-Dunstable-Houghton Regis, ready for the opening of the guided busway in September 2013. This view shows the steep climb out at the beginning of the busway.

Opposite above: Two other companies operate over the busway. Grant Palmer Passenger Services began operating tendered services at Luton in 2001. The owner's father, Stuart Palmer, had run buses in competition to Luton & District until selling out in 1994. Their service C ran between Luton and Beechcroft estate, Dunstable up to every 30min. Note the specially specified registration on this Scania!

Opposite below: The third company is Centrebus. This is one of five Scania N230UB buses with East Lancs Esteem bodies. They operated two services over the busway, routes B and E, although the digital blinds are not showing which route this is on.

Above: In 2015, Arriva the Shires bought a batch of these Wright Streetlite WF (wheel forward) buses 2511-28 which are operated on local services in both High Wycombe and Luton. Laying over in Luton town centre when new is 2521. These vehicles carry names – above the rear side window is written 'My name is "Hannan"'.

Opposite above: Luton & District bought the Green Line route 757 from London Country (North East), taking sole responsibility of the route from 11 June 1988. At first the Luton & District livery and name was used but the Green Line identity was later returned. The route received five wheelchair-accessible coaches in 2006. In 2008, they invested £4m in sixteen Van Hool tri-axle Acrons with wheelchair lifts to operate the service. The 757 had become a major success story, now running at least every twenty minutes, 24 hours a day. Booking though easyBus and Terravision meant that overseas visitors could book seats on the coaches before flying. The Acrons initially carried Green Line livery but later some were repainted in easyBus orange or, as here at Victoria in 2011, into a hybrid style.

Opposite below: Grant Palmer began running double-deck buses on the Luton busway in 2017 in the form of ex-Go-Ahead London Volvo B7TLs with Wright bodywork. This is at the station interchange. They added route CX in 2018 to the White Lion Retail Park in Dunstable.

Above: Luton Airport does not just get coach connections from London. Stagecoach run route 99 every thirty minutes in from Milton Keynes with route-branded coaches.

Below: The first MCV EvoRa-bodied Volvo B8RLEs for a UK operator entered service with Uno on route 610 Luton-Cockfosters in 2018. The route is branded as 'Dragonfly'.

AYLESBURY

Aylesbury was one of those nodal towns where several operators met up. As well as LT/LCBS working in, United Counties had a garage here and City of Oxford also had routes into the town.

A local independent company was Red Rover, also trading as Keith Coaches. They had started out in the 1920s. An express service to London had been acquired by London Transport to become a Green Line route. By deregulation in 1985, they were operating a number of town and country services around Aylesbury, a free service to a Tesco store and several school contracts. After deregulation, some new routes were won on tendering while others were lost or dropped.

New routes saw them reaching Chesham and Luton on the London Country boundary, and a Sundays Chiltern Rambler service brought their buses to Hemel Hempstead. From May 1987, they also won tenders for local and Sunday routes in Milton Keynes. However, Red Rover would pass to Luton & District at the end of January 1988. The name was initially retained, being applied to various Luton & District vehicles.

Although Arriva, as successors to Luton & District, still run several routes into Aylesbury, by 2018 cutbacks had left them with just one town service, with all the others being in the hands of independent companies.

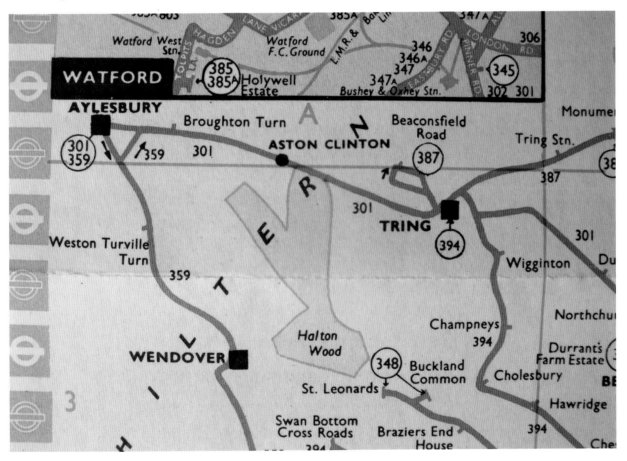

Aylesbury area Country Area services 1969.

Above: London Country Green Line modified RF178 of 1952 lays over at Aylesbury. The blinds have been set for the long cross-London trip to Chelsham. The bus carries a TG (Tring) garage plate. 18 September 1971.

Below: One of the older vehicles still in the United Counties fleet in 1971, 945 is a 1954 Bristol KSW6B with ECW L27/28R bodywork. On 18 September it was working route 369 to Stoke Mandeville Hospital.

Above: Local operator Red Rover worked a mix of town services and some country routes. AEC Bridgemaster 6116 BH was bought new in 1963, a diverted order from Baxters, Airdrie, also seen on 18 September 1971. This was withdrawn in 1977.

Below: AEC vehicles were also the choice for Red Rover single-deck buses in the 1960s. While several were bought new, EPH 189B, a 1964 AEC Reliance with Duple Midland body, came from another independent bus operator with town services – Safeguard of Guildford in 1971.

Above: Oxford acquired 1963 Daimler Fleetline/Alexander buses 908-23 from Midland Red. No. 909 (5273 HA), formerly Midland Red 5273, arrives at Aylesbury in September 1974. The company adopted the Oxford/South Midland fleetname after the South Midland fleet (which operated the services from Oxford to London) was transferred from Thames Valley ownership from 1 January 1971.

Below: Sporting a modernised livery, Red Rover 166 (OKW 515R) stands outside Aylesbury station on 6 September 1987. This was working a shuttle service to the Showbus Rally, held at Woburn Abbey that day. Although visually similar to London Transport's DMS class Fleetlines, this MCW bodied example was from a batch new to South Yorkshire PTE (fleet number 1515).

Above: A former United Counties VR in Luton & District colours and with the local 'Aylesbury Bus' fleetname in 1992.

Below: Working a local service the same day is Motts, Stoke Mandeville, C52 HDT. This is a rare Dennis Domino originally with South Yorkshire PTE. Their bus services passed to Luton & District in July 1995.

Above: Also in 1995, Luton & District became sole operators of the 280 between Aylesbury and Oxford via Thame, previously shared with the Oxford Bus Company. In 2013, this trunk route, now worked by Arriva as successor to L&D, was given the new premium 'Sapphire' status with the 2008-built Alexander Dennis Enviro400s refurbished and fitted with improved seating. This and other Sapphire routes elsewhere also had Wi-Fi sockets fitted, next stop audio announcements and dedicated uniformed drivers. Of four trial routes across the country selected for this treatment, the 280 was the best performing, achieving 18 per cent growth by 2015 when two extra new buses were added such as No. 5464, seen leaving Oxford for Aylesbury when new.

Opposite above: Red Rover have long gone, but Aylesbury is served by three 'red' companies – Red Rose, Red Eagle and Redline, each of which runs both local and county routes. Oldest is Red Rose whose red and yellow livery recalls that of Red Rover. While Alexander Dennis Darts are the main type in all three fleets, Red Rose have five of these 2006 Scania N94UB buses with East Lancs Esteem bodies at the time of writing. These came from Metrobus in 2019 and carry different colours around the blind box for different local routes.

Opposite below: Another company running services in Buckinghamshire and Oxfordshire is Z&S Buses. They have one Aylesbury local service, the K1, on which this Dart with its dedicated livery is running.

HIGH WYCOMBE

High Wycombe was another boundary town with a pattern of services by Thames Valley and LCBS as successors to London Transport that had remained largely unchanged since 1933. On 20 March 1970, a new bus station opened, served by these two companies.

In 1980, services in South Buckinghamshire around High Wycombe, Amersham and down towards Slough, Windsor and Reading were recast following the NBC MAP carried out in autumn 1978. The revised services operated by LCBS and Alder Valley (as successors to Thames Valley) were branded as 'Chilternlink' and all former Alder Valley routes were renumbered in the 300 series, as used by LCBS.

Alder Valley, having been created as a merger of Thames Valley and Aldershot & District in 1972, would be split back into its separate parts as Alder Valley North and Alder Valley South in 1986. Alder Valley North was then renamed the Berks Bucks Bus Co. from 25 January 1987, trading as 'Bee Line'. This company would be privatised in December 1987, being sold to Q Drive Ltd., a company set up by Len Wright Travel.

The High Wycombe operations of Berks Bucks Bus Co. (originally Thames Valley) were absorbed by the Oxford

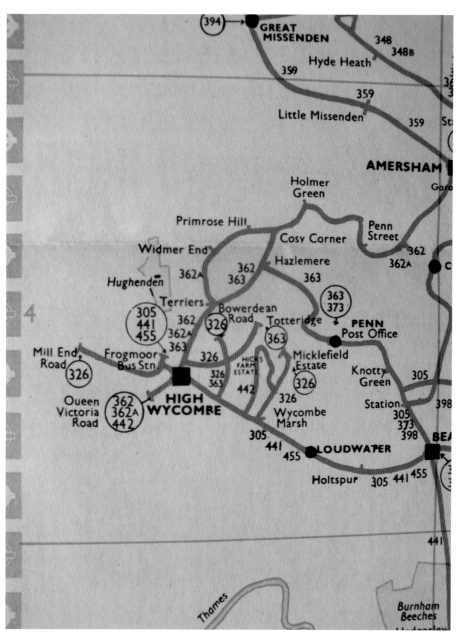

High Wycombe area Country Area services 1969.

Bus Company in October 1990 and operated as a separate unit, Wycombe Bus Company, with fifty vehicles. This incidentally brought Leyland Nationals to the company for the first time as Oxford were unique amongst NBC fleets in not purchasing any new. Oxford Bus Company had originally been sold to a management-led team but was sold to the Go-Ahead Group on 1 March 1994.

However, in December 2001 the Wycombe Bus Company and fifty-two vehicles were sold to Arriva the Shires & Essex for £5m. This was prompted by a compulsory purchase order placed on the company's bus station and depot as part of a redevelopment of the town centre which included a new bus station. As the only suitable site for a replacement depot was next to Arriva's depot they decided 'it therefore made more sense to dispose of the business and allow Arriva the opportunity to develop a fully-integrated service network for High Wycombe'.

The new £300m Eden shopping and leisure complex opened on 13 March 2008, although the new bus station built as part of this had opened eighteen months earlier.

London Country RML2412 at High Wycombe garage in May 1973. This has received the then new NBC green livery and fleetname style. This Routemaster is one of many that has now been preserved. The garage closed in 1977.

Above: Following the division of London Country, when this photo was taken on 18 April 1990 Leyland Atlantean AN235 had passed to London Country (North West). It carries a rather worn looking 'Chiltern Link' label.

Opposite above: Berks Bucks (Bee Line) 405, one of five Leyland Lynx buses added to the fleet in 1989. Route 326 was a town service, which along with the 303 was operated jointly with London Country (North West) at the time. Taken on 18 April 1990, these buses would pass to the new Wycombe Bus Company in November 1990. The ex-Berks Bucks vehicles had 1000 added to their numbers so this would become 1405.

Opposite below: Sporting the Oxford Bus Company livery and Wycombe Bus fleetname in 1994 is Bristol VR 1508. This did not come from Berks Bucks but was a second-hand addition to the fleet, having originated with Mayne's of Droylesden, Manchester. Route 328 to Reading was operated jointly with Reading Transport.

Above: Fleet No. 1117 was a 1984 Leyland Tiger with Plaxton Paramount C50F body. As can be seen, this was branded for route X80 from Aylesbury to Heathrow Airport via High Wycombe. Taken in 1994.

Opposite above: Bee Line still had a presence in High Wycombe at this time as seen by this Plaxton bodied Dennis Dart which has worked in from Slough.

Opposite below: Motts Travel originated in the 1950s. They expanded by takeovers and after the demise of Red Rover in 1988 they became the largest independent company in the area. Stage service operation did not begin until after deregulation, when in 1991 they began the M1 from High Wycombe to Aylesbury. Further expansion took place with tendered services from Oxfordshire CC out of Aylesbury and tendered services around High Wycombe, as well as some services operated commercially. TGD 219R, a Duple-bodied Leyland Leopard new to Grahams of Paisley, was taken in 1994. Some journeys on the M1 had been extended beyond High Wycombe to Lane End via Booker as is the case here and later on some journeys were extended to Stokenchurch and Reading via Watlington. Motts bus services were bought by Luton & District on 24 July 1995, the company continuing with coaching work.

Above: Seen in 1995, Luton & District AN244 was one of a pair of Leyland Atlanteans with ECW bodywork that had started out with Ribble in 1979. This is carrying the Chiltern Bus name used by both Amersham and High Wycombe depots.

Opposite above: Prestwood Travel, Great Kingshill, were a small company mainly engaged on school work but did have a route from Great Missenden into High Wycombe. CPE 480Y was one of two Leyland Leopards with Wadham Stringer B54F bodies. This was taken in 1995.

Opposite below: Luton & District 30 is one of three long-wheelbase Northern Counties bodied Leyland Olympians that came from London Country (North West). However, they were new to Ensign, Purfleet for London sightseeing work, before being sold to LCNW after a mere six months or so. All were allocated to High Wycombe. This is shown in the new livery adopted in 1995 and with the local Chiltern Rover fleetname for High Wycombe based vehicles.

Above: Wycombe Bus acquired fourteen of these Alexander-bodied Mercedes-Benz 811D buses from London Central. No 715 crosses the railway near the station in 1998.

Below: Some of the first batch of Dennis Dart SLFs for the Oxford Bus Company were allocated to the Wycombe Bus subsidiary in 1996, where No. 422 is seen later in 1999.

Above: Oxford's Wycombe Bus fleet acquired ten Dennis Darts from fellow Go-Ahead fleet London Central/London General in 1999 to replace Leyland Nationals. After the sale of Wycombe Bus to Arriva the Shires & Essex, one of these is seen in 2001 sporting the new owner's fleetname on the old livery.

Below: Carousel, High Wycombe, began in 2000 and have become major operators in this area. They bought Leyland Lynx buses F558/9 NJM in 2002 from Arriva the Shires. This was their fourth owner, while remaining based in the same town. They were new to Bee Line, then Wycombe Bus before Arriva and Carousel. This is seen at Heathrow Airport on new route A40 (named after the main road it used) from High Wycombe on 6 August 2003.

Above: New vehicles for Carousel's A10 route in March 2004 came in the form of three Mercedes-Benz Citaros partly financed by British Airways Authority. The route, run commercially, operated non-stop from Heathrow to RAF Uxbridge.

Below: Carousel Buses Dart/Plaxton DPL479 carries a green County Rider livery when working on Buckinghamshire tendered route 2 to Marlow. 9 June 2007.

Above: Arriva the Shires 3702 was a VDL SB120 with Wrightbus Cadet B39F body. This and 3701/3 carried a dedicated livery for the Cressex Park & Ride service which started in 2005. 9 June 2007.

Below: A very rare design in the Carousel fleet was the Irisbus Agora Lines, of which they had three examples dating from 2006. Irisbus was a name created when Iveco and Renault merged their bus manufacturing businesses in 1999 and was dropped in favour of Iveco Bus in 2013. This was AL3. They seated 44 passengers in a 12m long body and were normally used on route 4 to Chesham, which competed with Arriva route 362. These were the only such vehicles to be found anywhere in the area covered by this book. 7 June 2008.

Above: Two early production Optare Versas came to Arriva the Shires & Essex in 2007 painted in an orange livery for local routes 38/39. 2401 was on route 39 in June 2008. These routes would later pass to Carousel Buses in 2012 who also employed buses in a dedicated orange livery.

Below: Carousel Buses have been part of the Go-Ahead Group, managed jointly by Oxford Bus Company since 4 March 2012. The fleet was renumbered into the Oxford sequences and vehicles transferred to them from Go-Ahead fleets to replace many of the wide variety of unusual vehicles in the Carousel fleet such as the three Irisbus Agora Lines. From Oxford came eleven Dennis Tridents with Alexander bodies such as 112, taken on 24 March 2015.

Above: Arriva the Shires No. 3741 is seen outside High Wycombe railway station in 2015. This was one of seven 2006 built MAN 14.220 buses with MCV Evolution bodywork. These were branded for route 1 to Chesham although this is on the 31 on this occasion.

Below: Vale Travel is a small operator based at Aylesbury although most of their routes are in the Milton Keynes area. In 2015 they also had the Monday-Friday route 27 and Sunday 48/48A around High Wycombe and this Alexander Dennis AD E200 Dart was the regular vehicle used.

Above: Arriva introduced 'Sapphire' and 'Max' brandings for some of their more important routes from 2013. One route treated to the 'Max' branding was the 300 from Aylesbury to High Wycombe. Mercedes-Benz Citaro 3922 nears the bus station in 2015.

Below: First Berkshire is the current successor to Thames Valley, Alder Valley, Bee Line, etc. Backing out of the bus station in 2019 and departing for Slough is 63313, the first of five Wright StreetLites bought in 2015. This has route branding for this service.

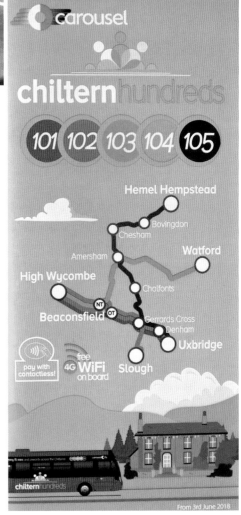

Above: Carousel Buses are now a major operator in High Wycombe with routes to Chesham, Thame, Slough, Watford and Uxbridge amongst others. 873 was one of three unusual Mercedes-Benz OC500U buses with MCV Evolution bodies. It carries the 'Chiltern Hundreds' branding introduced in June 2018 for revised routes 101-5 and is backing out of the bus station on 1 September 2019. This was the date of a 'Running Day' in High Wycombe hence the appearance of a preserved London GS type in the bus station. The 101/2 replaced the A40/740 services to Uxbridge with the extension to Heathrow withdrawn, although Heathrow journeys were reinstated from December 2019.

Right: Carousel Buses Chiltern Hundreds leaflet 2018.

SELECT BIBLIOGRAPHY

AKEHURST, Laurie, and STEWART, David, *London Country 2nd edition* (Capital Transport, 2001)

BEDDALL, David, *Luton's Transport* (Pen & Sword, 2022)

DELAHOY, Richard, *Glory Days: Eastern National* (Ian Allan, 2003)

FENNEL, Steve, *London Country in the 1970s* (Ian Allan, 2003)

KING, Nicholas, *London Bus Handbook Part 1: London Buses Ltd.* (Capital Transport, various editions 1990s)

KING, Nicholas, *London Bus Handbook Part 2: Independents* (Capital Transport, various editions 1990s)

McCORMACK, Kevin, *London's Country Buses* (Capital Transport, 2020)

WALLIS, Philip, *London Transport Connections 194 –1985* (Capital Transport, 2003)

PERIODICALS AND WEBSITES

Buses (monthly magazine) (Ian Allan, 1949 onwards, now Key Publishing)

www.harlowride.co.uk

The London Bus (monthly newsletter) (London Omnibus Traction Society)

Various fleetlists published by The PSV Circle, Capital Transport, London Omnibus Traction Society, etc